In Pursuit of the Yellow Jersey

Greenwich Council
Library & Information Service

Neatly fix li here please

**Woolwich
Centre
020 8921 5750**

msc

RS

Please return by the last date shown

Thank
You!

To renew, please contact any Greenwich library

Issue: 02	Issue Date: 06.06.00	Ref: RM.RBL.LIS

D0412269

N.N.

In Pursuit of the Yellow Jersey

Bicycle Racing in the Year of the Tortured Tour

Samuel Abt and James Startt

Photographs by James Startt

Facing page: Ordinarily, French rider Damien Nazon
is a sprinter. But in the 1998 Tour de France he held
the dubious distinction of being the "Lanterne
Rouge," the last-placed rider. Nevertheless he
dug in deep to finish.

A CYCLING RESOURCES book
published by
Van der Plas Publications
San Francisco

Copyright © 1999 Samuel Abt and James N. Startt
Text and cover printed in U.S.A.
Color photo insert printed in Italy

Published by:

Van der Plas Publications
1282 7th Ave.
San Francisco, CA 94122
U.S.A.

U.S. book trade sales:

Dan Haldeman & Associates
Watsonville, CA

Cover design:

Rob van der Plas, based on a photograph by James Startt
of Marco Pantani in the Yellow Jersey at the Arc de Triomphe in Paris
on the last day of the 1998 Tour de France.

Photography:

James Startt (photos in text, front cover, and color insert)
Craig Cook (author photos on back cover and page 6)

Publisher's Cataloging in Publication Data

Abt, Samuel
In Pursuit of the Yellow Jersey: Bicycle Racing in the Year of the
Tortured Tour. Samuel Abt and James N. Startt.
p. cm.   Includes index.
ISBN 1-892495-16-3 (paperback)
1. Bicycle racing. I. Startt, James N. II. Title.
L.C. Card No. 98-75020

For Becky

About the Authors

Samuel Abt (right) has written about bicycle racers and racing since 1978 for the *New York Times* and the *International Herald Tribune*, where he is associate editor. Among his previous seven books about the sport are *Breakaway*, *In High Gear*, *Tour de France*, *A Season in Turmoil*, and biographies of Greg LeMond and Miguel Indurain.

"His words are like liquid gold," says a fan, former Prime Minister Romano Podi of Italy. Mr. Abt has his detractors too.

A graduate of Brown University, where he majored in English and American literature of the 19th Century, he has also been a professional Journalism Fellow at Stanford University, where he studied history. He is the only American to have been awarded the Tour de France medal for service to the race and the sport.

James Startt (left) is a Paris-based photographer and writer who has followed the Tour de France and other cycling events for the last decade. His stories and photographs have appeared in most English- and French-language cycling reviews around the world, as well as in such daily newspapers as the *Christian Science Monitor* and the *Philadelphia Inquirer* in the United States and *Le Parisien*, *Libération*, and *L'Equipe* magazine in France.

Startt exhibits his photographs regularly, and his pictures are represented by the Agathe Gaillard Gallery in Paris. A selection of his work was included in exhibits at the Photo Biennial of Montpellier and the Milwaukee Art Museum during the summer of 1998. In the same year, the Bibliothèque Nationale in Paris purchased ten of Startt's color photographs.

Since 1998, he has been the editor of the English version of *Le Site Official*, the official Tour de France Internet site. He is currently working on a history of the Tour de France, to be published by Chronicle Books in 1999.

Acknowledgments

Our thanks to the many people who have helped in the reporting and writing of this book. Primarily among them are Rob van der Plas, Steve Wood, John Wilcockson, Rupert Guinness, Beth Schneider, Tim Maloney, Paul Sherwen, Phil Liggett, Anne-Sophie Bolon, Peter Berlin, Charley Cupic, Lionel Chami, Gilles Comte, Olivier Haralambon, Rob Arnold, Chris and Kathy Gutowsky, Phillip Heying, Agathe Gaillard, the many journalists of *L'Equipe*, and the Société du Tour de France. We would also like to thank John, Phoebe, and Claire Abt, and James and Cathy Startt.

Table of Contents

Table of Contents

Chapters 1, 33, 43, 54, 55, 56, 57, 58, and 59 by James Startt;
all other texts by Samuel Abt.

Prologue:
Voices in the Crowd

"WHAT about the Festina scandal?" demanded the man standing under the banner that read *Salins, Jura, with Cédric Vasseur*. "Who cares about the TVM scandal?

"Listen, my friend," he continued to a man he first met two minutes before, "drugs and doping are not what the Tour de France is all about. The Tour de France is about Cédric Vasseur, you and me. The Tour de France is about sports and a good time. Forget doping, my good friend. Go eat some chicken."

The chicken—"not as bad as you might think," judged a man with a plate of it and French fried potatoes—and three kinds of sausages, each with fries, plus wine and beer, were all for sale at a picnic lunch organized in the town of Salins les Bains to celebrate the flypast of the Tour de France, including Vasseur, a Frenchman who had turned 28 a week before and who rode for the Gan team in the 1998 Tour.

Vasseur was not from the town, a porcelain center in the Jura, but from the north, at least 600 kilometers (390 miles) away. How he happened to have a 100-member fan club in Salins les Bains and why the club decided to organize the day's festivities, which attracted hundreds of people who did not belong to the club, testify to the enduring strength of the world's greatest bicycle race and the sport itself despite the doping scandal that enveloped them.

"The cycling public in Europe is an educated public and they do, rightly or wrongly, know what goes on and to a certain extent they've accepted that," said Graham Jones, a Briton who rode in five Tours between 1979 and 1987, and finished three of them.

Members of the Cédric Vasseur Fan Club, many of them eating lunch in a big tent with four long tables and an accordionist singing on the stage, expressed more than acceptance. Men and women, young and old, they were uninterested in discussing the expulsion of the Festina team from the Tour, the arrest of half a dozen riders, team coaches, doctors, and masseurs, and the confessions of five riders who started the Tour that they had used such illegal performance-enhancing drugs as the artificial hormone EPO.

"It happens, it happens," was a typical comment. "That's not why we're here."

"That side of cycling doesn't concern us," said Claude Meyer, an organizer of the club and the lunch. "We prefer to concentrate on the good side, people like Cédric."

Meyer, 47, met Vasseur, then 23, when he was an amateur in the Tour du Franche-Comte, and Meyer, as he put it, was "no more than a *cyclotouriste* and a big fan." Vasseur, he continued, is "un chic type," a swell guy, and they quickly became friends. Vasseur's father, a former professional rider, is also a chic type and a friend of Meyer's.

Both Vasseurs began coming to Salins les Bains for occasional races, and the fan club was formed. When Vasseur wore the overall leader's yellow jersey for five days in the 1997 Tour, Salins went crazy, Meyer said.

Vasseur was pretty happy himself. "It was fantastic," he said in an interview early in the next Tour. "My father won a stage in the Tour de France but didn't get the jersey, so I was first in the family. "It changed my life. People looked at me differently, they waited for me to ride past. This year

Fans at the Cédric Vasseur fan club wait patiently for the pack to pass in Salins.

I'm not expecting to win it again, but I'll try to do my best and do a good Tour de France. If it happens, OK, great."

It didn't, but Vasseur rode well, ranking 24th overall and fourth in the king of the mountains competition as the race ended.

"Cédric is giving it his best," Meyer said. "That's what the Tour is about, giving it your best, not drugs. All of this is in honor of Cédric and the Tour. Go look at the collection of old bicycles we have here, the old racing jerseys."

Salins is just another small town in France, seven kilometers from equally obscure Pagnoz to the west and six kilometers from uncelebrated Cernans to the east. For a few hours, though, Salins and the Place Aubarède, where the celebration was held, were the center of the small world of bicycle racing.

The Cédric Vasseur Fan Club Welcomes You, said a banner across the road, and the welcome was sincere as long as nobody tried to talk about illegal drugs. "How about a sausage, my good friend." the man said when the topic came up.

Vasseur addressed the issue after the 18th stage, when he finished 11th at the end of a long breakaway that ended in a mass sprint into Neuchatel, Switzerland.

"This is the third long breakaway I've ridden in that was caught near the line," he said. "Luck smiled on me last year, but not this one. The Tour is the most beautiful race in the world, and I owe it my glory and the most beautiful moments of my career. I owe it a debt.

"Many people go to a lot of work to organize this race, many people travel to our roads to applaud us, the riders accept many sacrifices to get ready for the Tour. It's a pity that the party might be spoiled. We all have to work so that the Tour remains a jewel of France's heritage. Sports must make that happen."

PART I

ALL ROADS LEAD TO THE TOUR

1. Spring Warm-Up: Saturday in the Park with Jaja

IT'S SATURDAY morning. Around the Longchamps Hippodrome in the Bois de Boulogne on the outskirts of Paris, the weekend crowd is out for its traditional spin in the park. There's a break in the dismal winter weather and the numbers are good. Most of today's peloton consists of what is known as "the stomachs," that cheery band of middle-aged fellows who visibly prefer serious eating and drinking to serious training.

But something is wrong with this picture. Tucked in the middle is a group of yellow-clad riders wearing ONCE team jerseys and riding team issue Giant bicycles. Now, plenty of "stomachs" wear similar store-bought copies of this jersey—after all the Spanish team is one of the world's best. But a quick double-take reveals that these jerseys are not bulging at the waistline. As a matter of fact, one would be hard pressed to find a single gram of excess fat among them.

This is the real ONCE team, and wedged in the middle is their star, Frenchman Laurent Jalabert. The team arrived early and the group is out for a light training ride to flush out any lactic acid that may have built up from the trip to Paris. Around the three kilometer circuit, word is out. "Heh! Régardez, c'est la ONCE, c'est 'Jaja'." Jalabert chats easily with the Saturday "stomachs." But then that is his style. He may be the world's number-one-ranked rider, but he remains a people's hero. Plus he's had plenty of practice with biker-talk; that nonsense-filled conversation, so removed from daily life that it actually soothes the spirit.

With ease and without irritation, he answers the same questions that he has faced all week prior to the defense of his third consecutive Paris–Nice title. "I really don't know how I'm going to do this week. I was in bed for three days last week with a temperature between 38 and 39 degrees (100 to 102 degrees Fahrenheit), but I can't stress out about it. How do the legs feel? Can't really tell. I haven't raced since I was sick. We'll find out soon enough."

Soon he hooks up with fellow professional Pascal Lino. Lino is now finishing out his career with the inauspicious Big Mat team, a second division French squad. But before Jalabert came into his own, before he dominated the world rankings, before he was adored by millions as Jaja, Lino was a star. His day in the sun came in 1992 when he wore the yellow jersey in the Tour de France for nearly half the race. As the two talk, the speed accelerates. From a leisurely 30 kilometers an hour (18 mph), the pack is now strung out at a spicy 40 km/h (25 mph). The "stomachs" shed from the Jalabert-led group within the space of a few hundred meters.

Jalabert remains motionless. He is relaxed, with his hands easily resting on the top of his handle bars. But despite his effortless pedal stroke, the speed continues to accelerate. Up the false flat, into a wailing headwind, he notches the speedometer over 45 km/h. Lino has sufficiently loosened up and he pulls off. After another lap, Jalabert eases. Looking around, he finally realizes that nearly everyone has abandoned his rear wheel. "Huh, no one left," he says to one hanger-on. "Guess the legs are all right. Ça va, heh?"

Laurent Jalabert cruises toward his team hotel in a down moment after a stage in the 1998 Paris–Nice race. He did not win that race that year but he was focused on other races later in the season.

"Yeh, ça va," Laurent. Throughout the whole test, his pulse barely reached a moderate 160 beats per minute. As he rolls around for another few laps, he again chats easily. Occasionally he hams it up with a mock sprint. He is definitely not preoccupied with Sunday's 10.2 kilometer time trial. "Yeh, I feel pretty good. But it is tomorrow when I really need to feel good. I'm not worried about it though."

One reason Jalabert appears so at ease is that he is not fixating on this early-season stage race. Sure the French press continues to compare his current Paris–Nice dominance with that of seven-time winner Sean Kelly—but not Jalabert. This year he is making a conscious effort not to be 100 percent in the spring. For once, he wants to focus entirely on the Tour de France. He knows that the world's greatest bike race hasn't smiled on him in recent years. He dropped out in 1996 and finished a miserable 43rd in 1997. Yet despite the setbacks, he is bucked up by his recent world championship time trial title and insists that he is just plain motivated by the big stage races.

Finally it is time for the ONCE boys to head back to the hotel for lunch and a final massage. Laurent dangles behind his teammates, gives the pack a wave and follows his team. Sunday's time trial may be the start of the first big race of the year, but that doesn't mean he can't enjoy Saturday in the park with the "stomachs."

At the end of the week-long Paris–Nice race, Jalabert rode plenty well. No, he didn't defend his title. That honor went to the up-and-coming Belgian Frank Vandenbroucke, who rode for the multi-national Mapei team. Unlike Jalabert, Vandenbroucke came into the race 100 percent. And after winning the prologue, he announced that this week-long stage race was one of his season's top priorities. Jalabert finished a respectable second. But then his main goals were further on up the road.

2. The Feisty Lance

THE FELLOW at the other end of the phone in April 1997 identified himself with a laugh as "a rider chump" and said he was in Italy, "just hanging out." It was Lance Armstrong, but a different one. This was not the somewhat solemn Lance Armstrong who found out first that his Motorola team—the supportive world he had known for four years—was collapsing, and then that he had testicular cancer that had spread to his lungs and brain, forcing surgery and chemotherapy.

This was not the Armstrong who, mid-January 1997, reported that the cancer was under control and that he was feeling good. He may have felt it then, but he didn't look it or act it.

Now this was the feisty Lance Armstrong, the buoyant one verging on brash, the Armstrong who won the road race world championship at age

A relaxed Armstrong chats with old friends during his mid-race visit to the 1997 Tour de France while waiting for the race to pass by.

21 in Oslo and consented to meet the king of Norway only if protocol was ignored and the rider could bring his mother to the audience with him.

He needed the name of a hotel to stay in Paris. "Near where the action is," he specified. "Maybe near the Champs-Elysées—lots of action there." There is, especially on that Sunday near the end of July when the Tour de France finishes its three-week journey there. Armstrong knows only the Tour de France's Paris: the Champs-Elysées, the nearby skyscraper hotel where the teams stay the night, the Tex-Mex restaurant in Montparnasse where his Motorola team traditionally celebrated the end of the race.

This time he wanted a small hotel, "lots of charm but not too expensive." He was traveling with a friend and training partner from Austin, Texas. Here was the number of his cellular phone. He was heading from Italy to Switzerland. Call him back, please, with suggestions.

A couple of hours later he was being given the name, address and phone number of a hotel on the Left Bank, near St. Germain. "Slowly," he instructed. "It's a little hard to drive and write at the same time."

Another complication: Instead of two rooms, he now needed maybe four. A representative of his sunglass sponsor had joined his group, and somebody from Switzerland was coming too, plus his manager, who was arriving from Texas. A pretty big party. "Party is my middle name," he said.

"Not really," he admitted a few days later. He and his troupe had checked into the hotel, walked around, seen the sights, had a few beers, and gone to bed not that late. He was in Europe not only as a tourist, but also to deal with some business.

First, he was looking for an apartment in the south of France to use as a base when he resumed European training. Second, the sponsor of his Cofidis team, which is based in France, wanted him to show up at a couple of races and press conferences.

"When the team says jump, I say, 'How high?'" he explained. He was at the Tour of Flanders early in April and would watch Paris–Roubaix and the Flèche Wallonne before returning to Texas.

The first two races did not mean that much to him, he said. Armstrong never has ridden well in Flanders and never competed in Paris–Roubaix because it is scheduled a week before the Ardennes classics, the Flèche and Liège–Bastogne–Liège, which rank among his main goals of the season.

In 1996 he had won the Flèche and then finished second in Liège–Bastogne–Liège. "It will be hard to watch the Flèche Wallonne," he knew.

First came the Paris–Roubaix appearances. He was seated now behind a table in a Paris hotel, being photographed by people who stood on fragile gilt chairs to take pictures of photographers taking pictures of him. He was answering familiar questions, the same ones he would answer again a few hours later in Compiègne, the start of Paris–Roubaix.

How does he feel? " I feel good, I feel normal." His hair, which he lost during three months of chemotherapy, had grown back and color had returned to his face.

Was he training? "The weather in Texas has been bad. I do two, three hours a day, but not very consistently. It's still something I enjoy, riding my bike. But I missed a day yesterday and it meant nothing. Last year, if I had missed a day, I would have been stressed out."

Does he have a date for his return to competition? "No. Not tomorrow. After the Tour de France, hopefully. It's only April and it hasn't been that long since I was very, very sick. I want to race, yeah, but I want to live. I'm waiting for the doctors to give me the go-ahead for hard training and hard racing. They would prefer that I hold off for this year."

Was the worst behind him? "I don't know. I hope so. I never was in pain from the cancer. I was sick from the therapy. Physically you get stronger, but mentally it's an uncertain time."

When was his next check-up? "The end of the month in Indianapolis. Every month you go to the doctor, and you never know what he's going to tell you. I do a blood test, a chest X-ray, and he looks at the X-ray immediately and sees if the tumors are gone. Then he calls the next day and tells me about the blood test. That's monthly in Austin. Every three months I go to Indianapolis for a CAT-scan and more extensive blood tests."

What did he miss most? "Absolutely journalists. No, I miss being with the team, the whole peloton, the whole sport—the fans, the masseurs and soigneurs, the give and take. It's truly a lifestyle and I miss that lifestyle."

And if he couldn't make a comeback? "Before, a big part of my life was the sport, doing well in my career. Now I realize that without cycling, I would still be extremely happy. Not that I wouldn't miss it, but I know now that the world revolves around getting up, being with people you care for. Before, I had to get up and I wanted to train—I got sulky if I didn't. Now I just want to get up."

Another viewpoint was provided outside the press conferences. "He's happy," said his friend and frequent training partner John Korioth, 30, the amateur racing champion of Texas.

"He's doing all the things he never had a chance to do before—taking his boat out, going to rock concerts, just seeing the bluebonnets come up. We've got a lot of bluebonnets in Texas and he hasn't been home in years to watch those flowers bloom. He asks me, 'What's going on this season?' because he hasn't been here. He's been somewhere else, racing his bike. Now he finds something to do near home. And that keeps him happy."

There's no question he's happy, Armstrong confirmed, much happier than he was at the team presentation in Paris two months earlier.

"The presentation was uncomfortable for me," he said, "because I hadn't been around the team, I hadn't been around the sport, and I didn't know what anybody expected. I looked bad, I looked sick. And they looked at me like I was sick. That's tough, when people look at you that way. Not that I really care, but it's as if they're afraid to approach you, afraid to touch you. And that's hard.

"Now I feel more normal. I'm much happier now than I was then, much happier than I was a year ago. I'm living a full life, full. Doing whatever I want. And if I don't want to do something, then I don't do it."

Just then his mobile phone rang. It was his friend and former teammate, Axel Merckx, the great Eddy Merckx's son, who was then riding for the Polti team in Italy. He was not entered in Paris–Roubaix but would be in the Flèche Wallonne.

They spoke about this and that for a few minutes. Then Armstrong told him: "Win the Flèche for me."

"Naw," he said quickly, "win it for you."

3. A Visitor

HERALDED by the hum of their wheels, the riders of the 1997 Tour de France were leaving Andorra, chatting and joking as they do before the daily battle really starts.

On the sidewalk, just before the riders turned a corner and began to pass out of sight, Lance Armstrong had stood, a spectator. This was not his battle now. It had not been since the previous October. He had not ridden in a professional race since then. He was sitting out the season because his doctors feared that arduous physical activity at that point might allow the cancer to recur. Armstrong joined the 1997 Tour as a visitor, participating mainly in a ceremony to honor his former teammate Fabio Casartelli, who was killed in a crash in the Pyrenees two years before.

Lance Armstrong hard at work during his first career. He is shown here climbing Beech Mountain during the 1996 Tour DuPont.

"It's a strange feeling but I'm comfortable just being a spectator right now," he said while he spent two days with the race. "It's not difficult for me…" He slowed and chose his words carefully, "… to come and watch."

Even when the thought was that banal, Armstrong was unaccustomedly slow to respond to some questions. Often the reply was full of uncertainty, as he was.

"It's kind of wait and see," he said of his future. "I'm still being monitored every month and so far, so good." His blood was last checked for signs of disease two weeks before in Austin, Texas, where he lives. Early in August, he went to Indianapolis for his three-month checkup and in-depth tests.

"My doctors have told me to rest this year," he said. "Whatever happens after this year, it's going to happen. I still consider myself a professional cyclist."

He had a deadline to know how long he would retain that status. "It's October," he said, "a year after I was diagnosed. The doctors pretty much dictate everything. Yeah, they do. The further I go there, the more clear my future will be: Whether I'll ride again, whether I won't ride again, whether I can ride again."

Being cleared to ride and wanting to do it are two different things, of course. Armstrong knew that a year off his bicycle, except for intermittent training, would not be overcome quickly or easily. Although he had not gained much weight and looked fit and happy, he noted that his muscle mass had turned soft.

Asked if he had brought a bicycle with him to Europe for training rides, he looked amused. No, he said, he left it behind. "I've been training so hard," he explained with a big, self-mocking smile, "that I have to taper off for a while."

If he could not return to the top level of the sport, he often said, he did not want to return at all.

More important, he was watching his health. "I feel great, super. I really do. I feel better than I did a year ago." And, he continued, he was enjoying life.

"I'm having a blast," he said. "I'm doing exactly what I want to do." That incuded playing "a lot of golf" and visiting Spain with his girlfriend. He went to Madrid, San Sebastian, and Pamplona, where he watched the running of the bulls, before joining the Tour briefly.

Armstrong said he was living both day-to-day and long-term at the same time. "Absolutely. When I wake up, I try to live every day fully and all-out as best I can, but I'd be lying if I said I didn't think about what I'm going to be doing 10 years from now."

His options were varied. "I have a bit of a financial cushion," he said, "but I don't have the mentality to sit around and do nothing. I'll find something."

Those options include starting college at the University of Texas, minutes from his home in Austin. "I've thought about it a lot," he said. "Business is the logical subject. I could also study medicine because that makes a lot of sense for me, but it takes so long. I wouldn't mind studying law, but probably business. It's an option. I have a lot of options, though, and that's a nice position to be in. Riding again is an option, staying involved in cycling is another, with American industry people."

Which sounded best? he was asked.

"None of them sound bad," he replied guardedly.

But which was best?

After a long pause, he said: "Good question. Sneaky too." He meant that he knew he was being pressed to say whether he preferred to race again. "I don't know which sounds best. This is an uncertain time for me. I'm kind of floating in terms of my career, and my future, and my professional life, and my health.

"It's really uncertain, so until there's some certainty, I'm not going to force myself to think about the future too much." Not many hours later, he was standing on the sidewalk as the Tour began to whirr by and leave town, and then he was gone too.

4. Back to Square One

LANCE ARMSTRONG didn't get very far in the second race of his comeback, dropping out in the first stage of the 1998 Paris–Nice race, but not to worry, team officials said.

"A comeback takes time," said Johnny Weltz, the U.S. Postal Service's directeur sportif, citing the extreme cold and the strong winds on the course. In other words, it seemed to be just a bump in the road in what Armstrong calls his second career.

His first career was a pretty good one, wasn't it? It was, until the day in the fall of 1996 as he turned 25 that he discovered that he had testicular cancer. After intense chemotherapy through December of that year, he sat out the 1997 season. "It was a vacation," he says.

Armstrong continued working on his woeful golf game and traveling with his fiancee. He passed medical checkups, spent a week in a musical tour of North Carolina with Jakob Dylan and the Wallflowers, organized a foundation to promote cancer awareness, sat at his home in Austin, Texas, and watched the seasons change—even rode his bicycle occasionally. "In '97 I lived the life of a vacationing retired cyclist," he says. "And it was the greatest year of my life. Absolutely."

He was talking before Paris–Nice in a somewhat remote hotel in the even more remote town of Orgeval. A bright-lights, big-city guy, Armstrong had hoped to be closer to Paris than this hotel offering not much more than a view of the A14 autoroute.

"Nothing's changed," he grumbled. That was a good sign: In his first career, he often complained about the way bicycle teams are treated by race organizers.

In fact, everything had changed. Primarily it was the sight of Armstrong, fresh from his massage and shower, looking lean and race-ready in the casual uniform of the U.S. Postal Service team.

Not many people expected to see him racing again, especially after he visited the 1997 Tour de France and told friends how happy he was away from competition. Armstrong had no short-range financial problems, having spent his money conservatively, as he says, and invested it wisely. Why was he racing again?

"It was hard to come back," he said, "it was a big sacrifice. Before, cycling was my life, and I treated it as such. It was a job, it was a very hard job, and it was something I focused on 100 percent. For a year I just assumed it was gone. So mentally, for 12 months, I learned to move on, to live without cycling.

"Now, to come back, you're reintroduced to how hard it is, to how much focus it takes, how much time you're away from home, how dangerous it is.

"I'm not here for myself," he said, leaning forward in his chair for emphasis. "I'm not here for the sport, I'm not here to promote cycling in America. "I'm here for the cancer community. Bottom line. If it wasn't for them and the big question mark that was put on me and the doubt that was put in me, I wouldn't have come back.

"I think there's a lot to prove for a person that's been sick, that's been treated, that's recovering. I'm trying to prove it can be done. It's never been attempted. It's not as if there's been any standard set. It's never been attempted in an endurance-intense sport like cycling. Most people said it couldn't be done.

"I'm healthy, I'm representing a world of cancer patients, families of cancer patients, oncologists, researchers, everything. My situation was bad, very bad, and now I feel wonderful. And the best way to relate that is through my performance."

Those are what he calls the positives. There are negatives too. He was angry at the governing body of the sport, the International Cycling Union, or UCI, for not waiving part of its rule that strips a rider of the points he has won in a race if he does not repeat his results. In Armstrong's case, after a year away, he lost all 1,300 points that ranked him in the top 10 in the world.

His 15th place in the Ruta del Sol race in February gave him 13 points. "One percent of what I had before I got sick," he said scornfully. "I had zero. I don't expect to come back and be ranked fourth in the world but I don't expect to go from 1,300 to zero. It's absurd. Certainly there should be exceptions."

With no points to bring to a team and win it invitations to major races, he had a difficult time attracting interest for his return, especially when he and his former employer, the Cofidis team, agreed to disagree.

"We called teams," he said, "and yes, I have the name, and yes, I have past results, but I have no points, I have an incredible medical history, I have an unknown potential. There was no interest in me: Three out of 20 teams answered. Sure, maybe there is a part of me that is a little angry—angry at the sport."

He shifted in his chair, smiled and fluttered his hand. "Ah," he said. Back to positives.

Armstrong was happy with living and training conditions at his new apartment on the Côte d'Azur in France, he would be married May 8 in California, he was excited about the work his cancer-awareness foundation was doing, including a race he was helping to organize in Austin on May 22, followed the next day by a long bicycle ride for the public. Sponsors' payments, entry fees, and fans' pledges go to fight cancer.

Until then there would be races to prove that the disease could not stop him or other patients. Beyond this season, his plans were uncertain. "I'm certainly not signing any contract now for next year," he said.

"I have to decide a lot. First is if I've done everything I set out to do in the second career. The first career, I'm happy. I could walk away from the first career, results-wise. The second career, have I proven to myself and the cancer community that I can be competitive again?

"In a lot of ways, I've already done that at the Ruta del Sol. I can almost stop now. I set out to do what I want to do, and I was a lot closer to packing it in after Ruta del Sol than many people think. Just because I proved it."

5. Square Two

LANCE ARMSTRONG had his schedule worked out precisely: finish the Tour of Luxembourg in June 1998, drive for about an hour and a half from that country to the French city of Metz, and catch the last plane to Spain for his next race.

He missed the plane, though. What he forgot to factor in was the time needed for the ceremony—bouquet, kisses, handshakes, photographs—and the drug test that accompany a victory.

"I won!" Armstrong said excitedly. "It worked out. Oh, it feels great."

His ebullience after the four-day Tour of Luxembourg was understandable. The 26-year-old Texan had won some big races before, but that happened in his first career.

The result in Luxembourg, including a victory in the opening stage, was his first triumph in top-level competition in nearly two years. "It means something, it does, it does," he said.

Against broad expectations, Armstrong returned to competition for his new team, U.S. Postal Service, in February and finished a fine 15th in his first race, the Ruta del Sol in Spain. A month later, on the first stage of the Paris–Nice race, he suddenly quit and returned to Texas. He gave no explanation.

"I think I've worked out a lot of things" in the three months since, Armstrong said by phone from Metz. During the spring he resumed training, helped organize a mass ride to benefit his cancer foundation, was married, and resumed racing in the United States with some creditable results.

"That doesn't really count," he said of the American races. "This is a completely different level. I'm happier this time around. This feels more right, or however I can say it—this feels better than in February. Before Paris–Nice, I thought I could just leave at that point, and I did end up leaving. I don't have that feeling now."

He was unable to rank his latest victory among the other milestones in his career, he continued. "It's a different satisfaction. I don't think I can compare this to anything I did in my prior career. In my mind I have it in a different category. It feels like a second career and the engine feels like a second engine. My body feels different. But I have returned. That's such an important message to me and for the cancer community."

Armstrong rode next in the Tour of Valencia, followed by a race in Germany, which he also won, before he returned to the United States a week before the start of the Tour de France. "I'm racing 19 days out of the 23 I'll be here."

He would make no predictions about his results in the rest of his season. "I've won this race, but it's not as if I go to Spain and expect to win there. I completely know and understand that it's a different race and a different field."

So there was no point in wishing him well and hoping that the victory in Luxembourg was the first of many more?

"I won't say I don't hope so too," he replied. "But if it's not, it's not. Today has been great, but I've got to take everything in stride. I just want to go one day at a time."

Which is just what he did for the rest of what turned out to be an extraordinary season. In September, he entered the Vuelta for what was expected to be a short tune-up for the world championships, but he rode so well and climbed so strongly that he completed the three-week race, finishing fourth overall, just six seconds from the podium. In the world championships a few weeks later in the Netherlands, he recorded two more fourth places, in the time trial and the road race.

"Armstrong's the man of the year," said a longtime rival, Laurent Jalabert, during the Vuelta. "He's come back from so far down that you can't help admire him."

There was no quarreling with that.

6. An Ardennes Classic

GEORG TOTSCHNIG's big adventure started shortly after 10 A.M., a bit less than five kilometers into the Liège–Bastogne–Liège bicycle classic, in the town of Beaufays, just outside the city limits of Liège, as the riders were moving gently uphill and trying to generate a little warmth for themselves on a cold morning.

Probably people were still chatting in the pack, as the riders do when they are moving out, still going nowhere.

The 188 riders did have a destination, of course. First was Bastogne, deep in the Ardennes and a key site of the Battle of the Bulge in World War II, when encircled American troops held the town during December 1944 and January 1945 and stopped German tanks that were attempting to break the Allied lines and thrust to Brussels and beyond. After Bastogne, the destination was the same Liège the pack had just left.

Liège–Bastogne–Liège is the oldest of the sport's one-day classics, started in 1892 and run nearly every year since, except for a few years at the turn of the century and then again during World War I. During World War II, it was held in 1943 as a sign that all was normal in Belgium under German occupation.

It is a demanding race, including a dozen of the short but steep hills that keep the country from being flat as a table. Nobody in living memory has won Liège–Bastogne–Liège with a breakaway from start to finish, since the route is 262 kilometers (163 miles) long, the winds usually strong, and those hills murderous on tired legs.

But the lack of success on long breakaways has not curtailed them. Nearly every year somebody goes off on an early attack, builds a big lead, and then is caught 80, 90, or 100 kilometers from the finish, where the real race begins. In 1997 it was Totschnig's turn.

The Austrian rider was then 25 years old and ranked 79th in the computerized standings of the world's top 900 riders and had done nothing lately to move up or down.

In 1996 he recorded one victory, in the championship of Austria. The year before he finished a splendid ninth in the three-week Giro d'Italia and demonstrated climbing ability. He was hired by Deutsche Telekom to offer support in the mountains.

A worker bee, then, and nobody to get excited about if he attacked early in Liège–Bastogne–Liège, especially if he went alone and had nobody to take a turn setting the pace and sheltering him from the wind on the long trip south to Bastogne and then the return over most of those dozen hills.

By kilometer 26, he had a lead of 4 minutes 10 seconds. By kilometer 35, as he moved parallel to a long stream dotted with fishermen, his lead was up to 6:15. The fishermen were serious and had landing nets to prove it; most likely they were after brook trout.

Past apple and wild cherry trees in flower, past small herds of cattle in pastures, past dark hillsides posted against hunters and foamy brooks posted against fishermen, Totschnig flew. Fighting a headwind, he was moving at a steady 40 kilometers an hour, about 8 more than the pack.

The slightest sprinkle of rain turned to snow and, far behind him, the race radio reported team cars being called to the pack for riders who wanted another jacket. By kilometer 50, when his lead was at 11:20, the sky lightened in the southwest. By kilometer 69, Totschnig was being pushed by a tailwind and his lead, as he crested a long hill and had a view of the shadowed valley below, rose to 14:10.

In a field, a trough of water for cattle was covered with a film of ice. A roadside sign announced a deer crossing. At the first major hill, the Côte de St. Roch, 900 meters with a 12 percent grade, a big crowd of fans waited at the summit, kilometer 81. It was snowing lightly again.

Into Bastogne Totschnig came, turning right at the Patton tank that commemorates the battle there, and heading back north. He had already grabbed his musette with sandwiches, fruit, and cakes at the feed zone, kilometer 98, when another rider surged out of the pack, in pursuit.

Technically it was a counterattack, but the term sounded strange when the rider in front was ahead by 18:15. By whatever name, the chase was on. The chaser was Ermanno Brignoli, 27, an Italian with the Batik team, unranked by the computer in his fourth year as a professional, another worker bee. The pack let him go too.

Brignoli caught Totschnig eventually, although it took a while. The Austrian was far and away first over the next three hills, but looking weary as he struggled against the strong wind that shook the dark boughs of the Ardennes trees. By the third of those hills, the Côte des Hezalles, 1.1 kilometers long at a grade of 11 percent, his lead over Brignoli was down to 2:30, with the pack four and a half minutes farther back.

The sun was out now and the dark clouds of morning had turned to white puffballs. In the pack, riders were calling their team cars so they could return jackets. Looking weary, Totschnig responded to fans' applause by rising from the saddle and putting some extra effort into the next climb, the Côte d'Aisomont, kilometer 171, nearly 5 km long with a grade of 5 percent.

He was first by 50 seconds over his chaser and then, on a steep and sinuous descent, he was overtaken. Totschnig had been out alone five hours. Nobody ever wins Liège–Bastogne–Liège with a start-to-finish breakaway, but somebody usually tries.

At the next climb, the Côte de Stockeu, kilometer 178, just over one kilometer at a grade of 12 percent, Brignoli was the first rider over, followed by Totschnig and then the pack, 3 minutes back.

Not long after that, first Totschnig and then Brignoli were caught and the real race began. The exact spot was kilometer 193 of the 262, the start of the climb up the Côte de Rosier, 4 kilometers with a grade of 6 percent. There were still six hills ahead.

Brignoli never did finish the race. Totschnig did. He was 108th of the 112 riders who made it, 15:55 behind the winner, Michele Bartoli. For his victory, Bartoli, an Italian then with MG, received 100 World Cup points, or enough to put him into a tie for the lead in the 10-race competition; 200 points in the computer rankings, or enough to move him from fifth in the world to third; and 500,000 Belgian francs ($14,300).

Totschnig gained no World Cup or computer points with his 108th place. By finishing, however, he won the king of the mountains prize, 100,000 Belgian francs plus 10,000 more for each of the five hills he conquered. As the custom is, he shared the money with his teammates, keeping for himself the exploit.

7. The Little Corporal

HOPING to inspire his troops to boldness, Napoleon declared that every corporal carries a field marshal's baton in his knapsack. Be brave, seize the moment, attack—the emperor's maxim is still taught in French schools.

François Lemarchand, a corporal throughout his long career as a bicycle racer, carried that baton once himself. In the 1996 French championships, he and a rival, Laurent Roux, were far ahead of the chasing pack and nearing the finish line in a drizzle. As they turned one of the final corners, Lemarchand's bicycle slid out from under him on the slick road and he crashed into a wall. Dazed, he slowly remounted and finished 11th, 20 seconds behind.

"I was confident," he said afterward. "I thought if it came to a sprint, it would be 50-50 at worst. I imagined myself champion of France." Instead, the honor went to his Gan teammate, Stéphane Heulot, who overtook Roux after Lemarchand's crash and won the two-man sprint himself.

"My biggest disappointment." Lemarchand. said in 1997, repeating a question. "Now, yes. Last year, yes, but now even more."

By that, he meant that he would not have another chance. After 13 years as a professional, Lemarchand retired that September at the age of 37, the oldest man in the French pack. His last competition was the Grand Prix d'Isbergues, a second-level race in the north of France.

"Isbergues and then it's all over," the native of Normandy said a few days beforehand. "A few criteriums after, but…" What do criteriums—exhibition races—matter to a rider who started and finished 10 Tours de France and who believed that he could be the French national champion?

"I'm always asked what I think of my career, and that's a dark patch," he said of the crash. "And now it won't come knocking again." He laughed softly. "Not at all.

"I had the same thing happen in the Tour de France a few years ago, getting caught 50 meters from the finish. Those are big disappointments, the two biggest. If I could have pulled off those victories, I might have had another career. Win a Tour stage, the French champion—after that, well, you can talk, you know."

Instead his high points include a victory in a stage of the Route du Sud in 1988, a victory in a stage of the Milk Race in 1989, victory overall in the Tour de Vendée in 1990 and a stage victory that same year in both the Quatre Jours de Dunkerque and the Midi Libre.

Otherwise he was a support rider, a corporal taking orders from such generals as Stephen Roche, Greg LeMond, and Chris Boardman. Typically, he said that his biggest thrill in the sport was helping LeMond win the Tour de France in 1990.

"Bringing the yellow jersey to Paris," he said. "And to be in the spotlight when the team rode a lap of honor on the Champs-Elysées. It's exceptional. And my other great pride is to have finished 10 Tours out of 10. I never gave up. I don't think there are many who can say that." Roche, LeMond, and Boardman all stopped in the Tour at least once, he was reminded. "Exactly," he replied. "Stopped. Exactly.

"I was always modest in my expectations," he said, "modest, with some high hopes at the same time. I never took myself too seriously and that's what made me last so long. I did the greatest races in the world, really a high level. It's a source of pride for me, and it's not going to be taken from me now."

In addition to his 10 Tours de France, he completed both Giros d'Italia and both Vueltas à España that he entered.

Lemarchand did not expect a Hollywood ending to his career in Isbergues. No, he wouldn't win. "The physical side isn't super," he said, referring to an operation for a saddle sore that June that kept him from riding in the Tour. "I didn't ride for a month. No competition for a month, it's not possible to stay at the highest level."

His motivation was down too, he admitted. "Knowing that I'm stopping, that makes a difference. The minute I made the decision to stop, I pulled the plug. I used to train all the time, but since I made the decision to stop, I can't train.

"I was going to retire last year, but I had a good season and so I continued. This year, since the beginning of the season, I've felt a bit weary. I had some health problems, which I'd never had before, and that kept my preparation back. I did some races where I've always felt good, and I wasn't as good. Then you ask yourself questions. "Still, I have the feeling of a job well done," he continued. "It's a good page. Not everybody had this luck—those who work from age 20 in a factory."

Lemarchand was not quite sure what he would do once he hangs his bicycle in the garage. "I'd like to stay in cycling," he said vaguely. "Maybe not for a team, in cycling in general."

He was not thinking too much about his final race in Isbergues. "My only motivation," he said, "is to be at the start, to see my buddies, to enjoy the race's ambiance. What I would have liked would have been to finish while racing well, but it won't happen. I might even have to drop out of the race.

"I'm not a rider who's dropped out of many races," he said, "but now it's almost impossible for me to finish." As the corporal feared, he didn't. Be brave, seize the moment, attack—at Isbergues, Lemarchand's baton stayed in his knapsack.

8. Forty-One Years and Counting

"FORTY-ONE years," sputtered Albert Bouvet in his excitable way, turning even more red in the face than usual. "Forty-one years that I've been waiting."

Bouvet has been waiting that long to have his burden lifted, to get out from under the heavy sorrow of having been the last Frenchman to win the esteemed Paris–Tours classic. He does not say it, but he thinks it is a disgrace that no Frenchman has won Paris–Tours, an arrow through the heart of the country, since he did in 1956.

He sighed. "For 41 years, it's been a very sad story," he said at the start of the race in October 1997, wearing a badge that bore his name and his identification as the last French winner. "Very sad."

The race was 101 years old that year and had been dominated by French riders from the first year through the mid-1950s. Twenty-eight times a Frenchman has won it, second only to the Belgians' 37. But not since 1956. Since then the winners have included Italians, Dutchmen, Germans, Belgians, of course, an Irishman, and—can this be true?—a Dane and an Australian.

A Dane? Not a Frenchman but an Australian? Bouvet's eyes rolled. What next, an Eskimo? A Bosnian? "Impossible," Bouvet said, "not possible." He laughed bitterly. "Very sad," he repeated.

He was entirely sincere. Another man might glory in his reputation as the last French champion, but not Bouvet. He was always a team player. He is more proud of having served Jacques Anquetil in his first Tour de France victory in 1957 than he is of his own triumph in Paris–Tours.

The years ease from Bouvet: His thick white hair turns dark, his jowls and gut recede, he is again the trim, 26-year-old "Bouledogue (pronounced 'bulldog') de Fougères," his hometown in Brittany. He wears the glorious Mercier team jersey and he is riding Paris–Tours in a strong wind, as always, and is far back in the race.

He is not happy, he did not want to be here and he has lost a lot of money, he thinks. A short time before, he finished second in the Grand Prix des Nations, a long time trial, and was offered 60,000 francs (then less than $1,000) to race on the track in Rennes the day that Paris–Tours was held on the road.

"Sixty thousand francs, even old francs, you don't refuse that," he remembers. But his team insisted that he ride Paris–Tours, in which he finished 25th the year before, winning all of 5,000 francs. He was not angry, he insists; he was, after all, a team rider. The track is where he performed best—French champion in pursuit from 1958 through 1960 and again in 1962, silver medal in pursuit in the world championships in 1957 and 1959—but if Mercier wanted him on the road, onto the road he went.

Midway to Tours, some 250 kilometers (150 miles) from Paris, he is far behind when his directeur sportif pulls alongside in his car and asks Bouvet with some asperity, "You riding or not?" The rider is stung. "Ten kilometers later, I was at the front," he says.

About 40 kilometers from the finish of that Paris–Tours, on a short descent from a hill, Bouvet attacks with an Italian rider. They build a small lead, not even two minutes, before Bouvet leaves behind his accomplice ("He was no help, he did no work"). Alone, the Frenchman holds off the pack for 25 kilometers: "Near the finish, I was this close to dropping the adventure, to sitting up and letting them catch me. I didn't believe I could do it. With one kilometer to go, I was only 80 meters ahead."

At the line, he was perhaps two meters ahead, but ahead. Two meters, two centimeters—he won. His prize came to 700,000 francs. He never again came close to winning Paris–Tours, but which Frenchman has? In the last decade, none has been closer than fifth place.

When his racing days were over, Bouvet became a journalist, writing mainly about bicycle racing, and then an official of the Tour de France. Before he retired in 1995, he had risen to director of competition, which meant that his was the voice everybody heard on the radio linking the Tour, screaming at cars ahead of the race to move out of the riders' way, bellowing at photographers' motorcycles that he had taken their number for interference and he would speak with the driver later in the press room, yowling at one and all to clear the road.

Albert Bouvet was quite excitable, to tell the truth, but now in his retirement he is calm. Somebody else is in charge of keeping press cars and motorcycles out of sight of the race, and he is happy to be merely an honored guest.

Not this day, however, not the Sunday of Paris–Tours. He paced the street where the race started in the suburb of St. Arnoult-en-Yvelines. (The "Paris" part is as flexible as the "Tours"; in the last 20 years, the race has transmuted itself into, south-north, Tours–Versailles, Blois–Monthléry and Blois–Chaville, and north-south, Créteil–Chaville. Lately it is fixed north-south from St. Arnoult to Tours in the Loire Valley.)

French chances of victory were slight. Paris–Tours by whatever name is almost always won in a sprint and the best native sprinter, Frédéric Moncassin—the best even though he had not won a race that year—had already called it a season and was home near Toulouse. The second-ranked French sprinters were just that, second-rank.

"Maybe Nazon," Bouvet said, referring to Damien Nazon, the French sprinter who blew everybody away in the minor Tour of China two years before. "Maybe Jalabert," he said, referring to Laurent Jalabert, the top-ranked rider in the world and, more important, a Frenchman. Maybe anybody, as long as he was French. Please not another Italian, Belgian, German, Dutchman, Irishman, Dane, or Australian. Not a Swiss. Not a Samoan.

Six hours later, it was a Ukrainian.

In a two-man sprint, Andrei Tchmil, a Ukrainian who was born in Russia and was seeking Belgian citizenship, beat Max Sciandri, an Italian who now rode as an Englishman. In that stew of nationalities, there was not a French gene.

The highest ranked Frenchman was in 22nd place. The only one who had seemed capable of victory was Jalabert, who was in front alone with 35 kilometers to go and a lead of about 30 seconds. He held out for 20 kilometers before he was caught.

On the long and straight avenue de Grammont in Tours, the site of the finish, Albert Bouvet slowly got out of an official car to watch the finish. His head was low and his face strained. He seemed to have been weeping.

"I hoped," he said. "When Jalabert attacked, I thought it was possible. I allowed myself to hope."

An old man pushed up to him in the crowd and gave him a photograph. Bouvet looked at it closely. "Look," he said, "this was 40 years ago." The cream of French racing was in the photograph. "This one here, that's Louison Bobet," Bouvet pointed out, "that's François Mahe. Here, that's Anquetil. And here," his finger stabbing a rider with a big smile and a look of ease, "that's me."

He peered up at the sky and spread his arms wide. "Maybe next year," he said.

* * * * *

The next year it happened, after 42 years of waiting. With 25 kilometers left in the race and a group of 11 riders a little over a minute ahead, Jacky

Jacky Durand has reason to celebrate. He's just become the first Frenchman in 42 years to win the Paris–Tours classic.

Durand of the Casino team bolted from the group. In an official car near the front, Albert Bouvet's heart leaped.

Durand was a rider Bouvet appreciated. An aggressive attacker—most combative in the Tour de France a few months before—Durand had won the 1992 Tour of Flanders with a long breakaway that nobody except Durand himself thought would go the distance. His relentless style carried him to victory also in the 1993 and 1994 French championships and to three stage wins in the Tour. If there was a rider fit to carry Bouvet's nickname of "le Bouledogue," it was Durand. And, best of all, of course, he was French.

Only Mirko Gualdi, an Italian with the Polti team, could catch Durand, and the two of them rode together into Tours, nearly a minute up on their chasers. With 350 meters to go, Durand made his final attack of the day and rolled across the line first, punching the air, by two seconds.

"I knew it, I knew it," a tearful Bouvet said on the podium as he hugged Durand. "This year all the conditions were right. It's been 42 years since I won, my speed was 42 kilometers an hour, I attacked with 42 kilometers to go.

"The only thing that worried me was that I didn't know how good a sprinter Gualdi was. I was afraid of another bad surprise. But I did know what kind of rider Jacky Durand is, what a fighter he is, and I was confident.

"Forty-two years," Bouvet kept repeating. He was overwhelmed. His burden had been lifted.

9. Back in the Hospital

ALMOST nobody believed in Wilfried Nelissen's chances for a comeback. The second comeback, that is. For the first one, his coach, his teammates, his many fans in Belgium, above all Nelissen himself—they believed. By March 1998, the list seemed to have dwindled to just Nelissen, if even.

Listen to Walter Planckaert, the directeur sportif of Nelissen's Palmans team: "He's in the hospital again, another knee operation. He'll miss training for four weeks once he gets out. When he gets out, we don't know yet."

In other words, the rider would not begin training until April at the earliest, far too late to be ready for the spring races. No matter what his condition thereafter, his minor Palmans team would not be eligible for any of the big races of summer and fall.

The season had just begun, but for Nelissen it seemed to be over already. At age 28, even for a healthy rider, there were not many years left.

"It will be difficult for him," Planckaert judged. "Extremely difficult."

A teammate, Gert Vanderaerden, a Belgian like Planckaert and Nelissen, was also blunt. "It doesn't look good for him," he said. "I think it's not so good."

They both spoke in Sint Pieter's Plein, a huge square in Ghent, before the start of the Het Volk race. Staged over 202 kilometers (125 miles), 11 short, steep climbs, and stretches of cobblestones near the finish, the Het Volk opens the season in the north of Europe after a month of races in the balmier weather of Spain, Italy, and the south of France.

The Het Volk is a tough race, especially when the wind is blowing hard, as it was in 1998. As they say in Belgium, mainly when a Belgian finishes first, it takes a tough man to win such a tough race. Nelissen has won it twice.

The first time was in 1993, and he became the bright hope of Belgian bicycle racing at age 22. Everything seemed possible for a sprinter as fleet as he was: Because the Het Volk is run over much of the same course as the Tour of Flanders in April, he became an instant favorite for that classic.

But the day after his victory, as he rode in the minor Kuurne–Brussels–Kuurne race, he crashed, broke his collarbone and missed the classics.

Nelissen won the Het Volk again in 1994, and seemed one more time to be heading for the top when he also won the Belgian national championship that June. But, a week later, in the first stage of the Tour de France, as he sprinted for the finish line with his head down, he plowed into a French policeman who had moved onto the course to take a photograph of the approaching riders.

Knocked unconscious by the crash at 70 kilometers an hour, Nelissen suffered a concussion and had to be hospitalized. His Tour was over. His first comeback began.

Was he shy now when the sprinting began? "No, not at all," he insisted. "It's all over now." To prove it, he won a criterium in Belgium that September and a few weeks later the Grand Prix d'Isbergues in France. "That felt good," he said.

In 1995, he repeated his victory in the Belgian championships and was wearing the black, yellow, and red striped jersey the following spring. No Het Volk victory this time, but he was off to a good start until the Ghent–Wevelgem race early in April.

Somehow—even two years later, the circumstances were unexplained—as the pack rode single-file in a heavy wind, Nelissen hit one of the many thick wooden stakes that mark the side of back-country roads. His right knee was shattered, his thigh ripped open, his shin fractured.

Then began his second comeback. Not until February 1997, nearly a year later, was he able to resume riding his bicycle. By then, his Lotto sponsor had dropped him and he moved from the country's only major team to Palmans, a low-budget one. When the Tour de France was starting that July, the rider who once wore its yellow jersey was finally fit for his first race.

It was one of the small ones, called "kermesses," that nearly every village in Belgium sponsors on weekends. Among the riders from such unsung Belgian teams as Ipso, Spar, Home Market and Tonissteiner, Nelissen raced up main streets, out past flat farmland, and then back down main streets.

Even if the competition was not overly stiff, and even if his team convoyed him most of the way, Nelissen still astounded the sport that summer by winning a kermesse in Sint Niklaas. He seemed to be on his way back.

Late in January 1998, he went to Spain to train for the new season, with the Het Volk his first big goal. But, after a 100-kilometer ride, he returned to his hotel in tears from the pain in his knee. He rested, he tried to train again and could not. Late in February he had an operation to repair calcification in the knee.

Nelissen planned to give himself one last chance to see if he had a future as a rider, his friends said. They had to speak for him because Nelissen himself would not discuss his chances then. Several weeks later, at the height of the spring classics, he made the expected announcement: He was finished, he said, as of that moment, retired.

10. A Helping Hand

THE FILIPINOS said it never happened. No, no, no, they insisted, it was a misunderstanding.

"An exaggeration," said Julius Enagan, the team's trainer. "I don't know why people think this. Nothing like this occurred. Come, we speak to the rider." He summoned No. 186 on his six-man team in Le Tour de Langkawi bicycle race, Carlo Jazul, who was checking his bicycle in Kota Bharu, Malaysia.

"Did Bugno push you across the finish?" the coach asked.

"No, no, no," Jazul replied.

"You see." Enagan placed his right arm around Jazul's shoulders. "Bugno comes up to him in the race and puts his arm on him like so and he says, 'You're a good boy, a good boy.' But push him across the finish? It never happened. No, no, no. It is not allowed. The penalty could be severe."

Sitting on the tailgate of his Mapei team car, Gianni Bugno, the star Italian rider, was rubbing sunblock onto his face and nose.

Ciao, Gianni. Had he helped an exhausted Filipino rider make it across the finish line after the demanding climb in the Genting Highlands of Malaysia a few days before?

"No, nothing," Bugno said. His eyes darted left to right and back again. "Not allowed to push another team."

He was right about that—a rider may help a teammate by staying at his side and pushing him uphill or even across the finish, but similar assistance for a rival could too easily be mistaken for interference. The Filipino trainer and Bugno knew the rule book: Pushing an opponent costs each rider a fine of 200 Swiss francs and a time penalty of two minutes. That's a lot of time in a sport that measures stages in seconds.

So, no, no, no, it never happened. Yet a handful of people saw it happen about 750 meters from the finish, after a steep 18-kilometer (11-mile) climb. As Bugno rolled along, he noticed that a Filipino rider was struggling and near collapse.

Bugno turned his bicycle back down the road, did a figure eight, came up behind the rider, put a hand in the small of his back and pushed him uphill until they were close enough to the line for the other rider to get across under his own power. That elegant gesture kept his rival in the race.

Ciao, Gianni. This time the questioner brought along an Italian journalist to translate. It helped also that the Italian journalist was an old friend of Bugno's.

"Sure, I helped him," the rider admitted, looking worried that he might be overheard. "I did it because he's one of us. I don't know his name or who he was, not even his number. All I know is that he was in bad trouble. We have to look out for each other, no?" he asked.

A check of the records for the Tour de Langkawi's sixth stage showed that Jazul had finished nearly two minutes ahead of Bugno. Obviously he had not been the one who was pushed, so could deny it truthfully.

But the records showed that two other riders on the Philippines' six-man team—Arnel Querimit and Enrique Domingo—finished seconds behind the Italian. It would be nice to think that Domingo was the beneficiary of Bugno's generosity.

Flash backward to the airport in Kuala Lumpur, where the 150 riders in the 1997 Tour de Langkawi were waiting to be flown to the start in Sabah. Hanging out for six hours while tickets were distributed, security was cleared and the plane loaded, everybody was bored and growing irritable.

Bugno went for a stroll and passed the Filipino team members, who were sitting on the floor. The riders recognized him—two-time world road-race champion, winner of the Giro d'Italia, champion of Italy, second- and third-place finisher in the Tour de France—and jumped to their feet.

The amateurs rushed him, crying "Bugno, Bugno," and asked him to pose for photographs. First was a team picture with Bugno in the middle, then individual shots of each of the six riders and their handful of officials with Bugno. He remained smiling throughout.

Afterward, somebody asked a rider if he really knew who Bugno was or just that he was a foreign professional rider.

"Bugno, of course," the rider responded. "A great champion. Two times in the world championships. The Giro. The Tour de France. I know Bugno. He is in all our racing magazines. One of my heroes."

That rider, of course, was Enrique Domingo.

11. Not Much Luck

RUDY DHAENENS was right: He never had much luck. Driving to the finish of the 1998 Tour of Flanders, where he would have been a consultant for the Eurosport Belgian television channel, he lost control of his car, swerved off the road and into a power pylon. He died the next night in a hospital from head injuries, leaving a wife and two children. Dhaenens would have been 37 years old that week.

The Tour of Flanders was one of his favorite races, not only because he was a Belgian and a native of Flanders, but mainly because he finished second in the classic in 1990. Dhaenens had a special affection for races in which he had ridden well: second in Paris–Roubaix in 1986, third there in 1987 and fifth in 1985; fourth in Liège–Bastogne–Liège in 1990 and in the Het Volk in 1988; third in the Belgian national championships in 1985.

Usually he looked like one of the small boys who asked Santa for a set of trains for Christmas and instead got underwear and a book, but his plain face could light up when he discussed the few races he had won. The world championship in Japan in 1990 was the peak, of course.

Dhaenens and a Belgian teammate, Dirk de Wolf, managed to get out in front of the pack and, after de Wolf collided with the only chaser in sight, Dag-Otto Lauritzen of Norway, and left him with a disabled bicycle, the way to the finish was clear. Dhaenens won by a second or two.

There have been unlikelier world champions. Dhaenens had also won a daily stage in the 1986 Tour de France and came close to repeating in 1989. He broke away alone and was heading for victory when he entered the final curve, 400 or so meters from the line.

"I took the corner too fast, maybe, or something happened with my wheel, maybe, and I slipped," he explained in an interview the next spring. "I still don't know," he admitted.

His bicycle skidded out from under him and he was thrown to the ground. When he got to his feet and found that his rear wheel was mangled, he could do nothing more than scream with rage as the pack shot by. Instead of being an easy winner, he was the last man to cross the finish line. "It just happened, so what can you do?" he asked those months later.

Because of an injury to Sean Kelly, who would have been the leader of the PDM team in the 1990 Paris–Roubaix, Dhaenens had been promoted to that role, but he understood who he was—a dependable, unselfish rider of moderate talent, not a star.

"Laurent Fignon wins more than I do, probably because he expects more of himself," Dhaenens said, referring to the Frenchman who won the Tour de France twice. The talk turned to Moreno Argentin, the Italian who had finished first ahead of Dhaenens a week earlier in the Tour of Flanders.

"There are guys who aren't often good during the year but when they're good, they win," he said. "Like Argentin: When he's super, he wins. He's super maybe four or five days a year, but he wins four of the five times. I'm not like him. I'm always in the top group, usually in the front, but I never win. And that's what's important in cycling races. To win, you need luck."

He had that at the world championships four months later, but not for long afterward. By the end of the 1992 season, he had to retire from the sport because of medical problems.

Not much was seen of Dhaenens for the next few years. Then, in July 1997, he showed up in the press room at the start of the Tour de France, looking tentative. He was working in a slight job, perhaps as a television consultant, perhaps as a representative of a bicycle shoe or saddle company. He looked pleased to be remembered.

"We must talk," he said, "I'll tell you what I've been doing. I'll be with the race only a few days," he warned. But in the bustle of the Tour, those few days sped by and then he was not to be found. Dying on the road to a bicycle race—there are worse ways to go.

12. He Had Some Fun

ON THE FAR side of 30 since that June, Darren Baker was preparing in 1997 to end his career as a professional racer, to leave Europe and return to the United States and become a businessman, somebody in financial services. Baker, who has a degree in finance from the University of Maryland, and his wife were already looking for an apartment in San Francisco, not far from their home in Santa Rosa, California.

"I have more aspirations than being a bicycle racer until I can't physically do it any more," he said.

But first he knew just the farewell present he would like: "A victory," he said. "That would be a nice way to go, wouldn't it?" A consistently high placer and occasional winner in American races, he never won in Europe, where he had competed as an amateur and professional since 1991.

Baker was at home then in Girona, Spain, north of Barcelona, just returned from riding for the U.S. Postal Service team in the Tour of Holland and getting ready for the three-week Vuelta à España, the Tour of Spain.

"One last chance," he said. "I'll look for my opportunity, do my best, and hope. If not," he continued, "it's been fun."

Yes, it has, and fun is important to him. The bright and lively Baker is rarely seen without a smile, never less so than during races in the United States, where his mother, father, and wife often showed up with one and sometimes two small dogs dressed in a miniature version of Baker's team jersey. The dog barked, Baker's parents held up signs saying "Go, Darren," and he rode by, beaming.

Once he left Europe, the native of Chambersburg, Pennsylvania, was not tempted to continue riding solely in America. "It's time to get going with the rest of my life," he said. "We want to start a family. The big goal is to retire before I'm 50 with enough money to buy a sailboat and sail around the world.

"Races in America are familiar and comfortable and not quite as difficult as they are in Europe," he said, laughing at his understatement. He was speaking the day before the Paris–Roubaix race, about as tough as it gets in a one-day classic.

"I don't mind difficult races," he continued, "but I like to be at least a little bit competitive. I don't feel I'm very competitive here." He blamed an intense spring schedule of races and then a long layoff.

"As a professional athlete, you want to excel. I speak for myself: I want to excel at every race. If you can't do that, it takes away a lot of the fun. I love racing my bike. It's the most fun thing in the world—you can get out there and viciously attack guys and not get into trouble. And you can win doing it."

Lately, though, he had been a support rider, working for a leader. "I'm not usually given a role," he said, "just helping other guys."

When he turned professional in 1993, with the Subaru-Montgomery team, a lot was expected of Baker because he had been so promising the previous two years with the U.S. national amateur team. "I was strong," he said. "Most of the time I was just as strong as Lance Armstrong," his teammate, "maybe even stronger on the climbs. But he was always more hungry for the win than I was. I envied him. That guy, he's so driven. Strong as anything. But I was too. I could put the hurt on guys, ride away from them."

Then, early in 1993, after a few races in the south of France, he got sick and wound up in a hospital in Dortmund, Germany, with pneumonia and a chest infection.

"I had a high fever for about a week, above 105," he recalled. "I don't know, I never really made it back after that. Some people say I was pretty close to dying." After that week of fever and hallucinations, his chest filled with so much liquid that his left lung collapsed and his heart was pushed to the right side of his chest cavity. "I'm basically dying, wasting away," he said of that time.

Showing a scar, he told how he finally went into surgery. "They cut my chest open, put seven tubes in to drain the liquid, but it had coagulated, so they cut my side open and scooped two and a half liters of junk out. Ever since then, I haven't felt the same. I've had spurts where I felt good, but I've never seriously felt that I could stomp the way I did in '92. Every year I get better, but it's never going to get back to where it was.

"So I have some regrets. My career wasn't what it could have been. But what can you do? I've seen a lot of the world, I've met some incredible people, it's been a great journey."

The trip started more than a decade ago, when Baker was a freshman at the University of Maryland and running cross-country. "I got hurt a lot," he remembered. "It's a big transition from cross-country high school to college because you jump from 5 kilometers to 10 kilometers—the mileage just goes through the roof—and I raced with tendinitis, shin splints, a bad knee, or a bad hip.

"And every time I got hurt, the trainers would throw me on a stationary bike until I got better. I got bored riding inside, so I bought a bike to ride outside and met so many people in cycling and I realized it's a really neat sport."

After he graduated in 1989, he spent the summer racing, and then took a job as a sales representative for an industrial company and worked his Baltimore territory for five months. "But I kept seeing friends I had met the summer before and they'd say, 'I'm going to France to race,' and I'd be 'Oh, gee,' and another guy would say, 'I'm going to the Olympic Training Center in Colorado and I'm going to be on the national team,' and I'd think, 'God, I was just beating these guys all summer.' I didn't know whether I was ready then to work for the rest of my life without giving cycling a try."

With his parents' approval, he quit his job and raced half the next year as an independent, joined the Moghul-Bismarck team, and impressed Chris Carmichael, the U.S. national team coach, who invited him to join the team in the Tour of Mexico. That winter Baker worked at the Olympic training center himself and the next two years rode for both Spago and the U.S. national team.

"Cycling can be feast or famine, and it's kind of good to see the famine side early," he says of his days as an independent racer. "It makes you save your pennies."

"Overall," he continued, "I feel fortunate. I have a good education to fall back on. I want to pursue the financial markets—I can absolutely see myself doing that. I was really hoping to do the Tour de France, end on a good note, end on a bang, kind of go out fighting." But he was not selected for the U.S. Postal Service team there.

"That's all right," he said. "The Tour of Spain, that's not a bad hand of cards to be dealt either."

13. Missing a Good Time

WHERE Bobby Julich wanted to be that weekend was Vail, Colorado, where the U.S. cycling crowd was having its annual awards banquet, and where he was going to be honored as North American rider of 1997.

"For the first time in my career, I've been nominated for an award," he said, "invited to go, all expenses paid—it's 45 minutes from where I grew up, all my friends and family are still there.

"I've been in this sport a long time," he continued. "A lot of people have helped me. If you get to accept an award, you can't name every single name of the people who have helped you, but being at that dinner, I

Bobby Julich racing strongly on Stage 18 of the 1997 Tour de France. After an good third week and an eventual 17th place overall, the American finally understood that he could race with the best.

would have been able to shake hands with them. To be honored before all those people…" The sentence trailed off. He looked up, a little jet-lagged, from his cup of coffee.

Where Bobby Julich was speaking and spending the morning that December was Terminal 2D at Roissy-Charles de Gaulle Airport outside Paris, waiting for his flight to Bordeaux. He had arrived by plane a few hours before from his new home in Philadelphia and was heading to a five-day training camp with the Cofidis team.

The team had 22 riders, and the camp was broken into two parts of 11 riders each, with both Saturday and Sunday their overlapping days for all-important publicity photographs and a chance to meet new teammates.

For Cofidis, which was a first-year term in 1997, there were a lot of new faces. Most prominently gone were Lance Armstrong and Tony Rominger, the Swiss star, who retired and became a public relations spokesman for the team. Gone also was Cyrille Guimard, the directeur sportif, who was facing criminal charges in another bicycle matter. Cofidis, which guarantees credit to consumers, thought it better not to have a coach accused of fraud.

The most prominent newcomers were Francesco Casagrande, an Italian who was sixth in the 1997 Tour de France, and—in a manner of speaking—Julich himself. He started the year for Cofidis as just another face, a low-paid domestique, and rode so strongly in the Tour, finishing 17th and excelling in the last of its three weeks, when lesser riders collapse, that to many he now ranked as a co-leader with Casagrande. Co-leaders do not skip training camp, of course, not even to receive an award they yearn for.

"I'm disappointed," Julich said softly, tearing at a raisin bun. "But there was nothing I could do. No way I can skip the camp.

"I would have liked to be there," he said of the Korbel Night of Champions in Vail. "To shake hands and say 'Thank you' to the people who have helped me. You can read about yourself but it's that one night when everyone in cycling is there, and it's fabulous if you've won that award, especially to be associated with the guys who have won that award in the past."

He ran down the list since 1989, when the awards were begun: among others, Greg LeMond, Andy Hampsten, and Lance Armstrong—the cream of American bicycle racers. Armstrong, then 26 years old like Julich, had won the award three times.

"Lance has always been Lance," said Julich, his longtime teammate on U.S. national squads, Motorola, and Cofidis. "He's just so massively strong, a superman. With me, I think I've had to work a lot more for what I've accomplished—nothing compared to what Lance has, but I'm starting to."

His start began more than a year before, when he finished ninth in the Vuelta à España and wore the leading climber's jersey for half the race. Until then Julich had been a young and overlooked rider with Motorola, a racer so dogged by bad luck that he had to spend 1993 as an independent, a rider on his own, when his team folded and he could not land another job.

Those were bad times for a rider who finished fifth in the 1991 Tour DuPont, at the age of 19, and seemed to have a shining future. Two years at Motorola added nothing to his reputation until the Vuelta and an 11th place a month later in the world championship road race.

Cofidis, just starting in the sport, took him aboard at a minimum salary. Although the year did not quite rank as a breakout season, he began to show his potential: victory in the minor Tour de l'Ain, two stage victories in the Route du Sud and then his impressive performance in the mountains of the Tour, and a splendid fourth place in the final time trial.

Suddenly teams were calling him. After talking primarily with Deutsche Telekom and U.S. Postal Service, Julich decided to sign for two more years with Cofidis, which raised his salary considerably and assigned him a leading role.

"It's always fun to be the dark horse or come out of nowhere and perform," Julich said, as the airport loudspeaker announced the plane for Bordeaux. "It's going to be totally different to be expected to perform well. That's how world champions are born: When you're expected to come through with the goods, you do. Nobody was better at that than Lance. When the pressure was on, he was ready. That's what I've got to do—take it up another level. I'm comfortable with that."

14. Michelin Man

TWO OR THREE more Bratwurst, Herr Ullrich?" "Seconds on the Sauerbraten?" "Another slice of Nusstorte, Herr Ullrich?" "Again some Schlag on your coffee?"

The answer in every case appears to have been affirmative.

As the first German to win the Tour de France, Jan Ullrich, 24, was heavily in demand on the rubber schnitzel circuit in the winter of 1998. "Heavily" is indeed the word. By the time Ullrich had downed his last dumpling and began preparing for the bicycle racing season, he weighed about 10 kilograms (22 pounds) more than his usual 73.

It showed, too. "Did you see Ullrich in any of his early races in Spain?" a rival was asked that spring. "See him?" the rider echoed. "You couldn't miss him."

Compounding the German's problems was a series of illnesses that kept interrupting his training and then his racing. By the end of April, the situation so alarmed the French sports newspaper *l'Equipe* that it devoted a full page to the unfolding calamity.

Of the first nine races on his program, the paper noted, he had quit four, been unable to start two, and finished three—in 78th, 97th, and 134th places. In contrast to 1997, when he had already raced 36 days for a total of 5,528 kilometers, he had put in 24 days for a total of 3,484 kilometers.

Laurent Jalabert, the top-ranked rider in the world, was quoted as saying that to see Ullrich trailing the field "provides a rather pathetic image of a Tour de France winner." Laurent Fignon, twice the winner of the Tour, accused Ullrich of lack of professionalism and called his conduct "inadmissible." Jean-Marie Leblanc, the director of the Tour, said his attitude was "unworthy of a Tour winner." The editorial package included a photograph of Ullrich that resembled Bibendum, the Michelin man, on a bicycle.

Enough. Sweating off the suet in Spain, where he raced almost exclusively that spring, and in a three-week training program in the Black Forest, Ullrich was rounding into form and beginning to get some results by June.

When the German arrived with his Telekom team in Chambéry for the one-day Classique des Alpes that month, he was fresh off a second place in the time trial in the Tour of Castille-Leon and a third place overall. There was still some poundage hanging over his belt buckle, but his face was once again lean.

"Maybe now we have to deal with three kilos too much," said Rudy Pevenage, 44, a Belgian who serves Telekom as assistant directeur sportif and Ullrich's confidant and spokesman. Ullrich himself gave one and all the same interview about his weight, his condition, and his goals—"Nein," which, while rich in nuance, does not survive translation.

Pevenage was unworried, he insisted. "It's still five weeks to go to the Tour, and in five weeks, three kilos is no problem. He's now at a very good level—80 percent, maybe 75—and after these five weeks, he'll be at 100 percent. I'm sure."

How had Ullrich managed to put on so many pounds during the winter? Did nobody from Telekom management keep an eye on him as he traipsed from banquet to banquet?

"It's not so easy," Pevenage said. "It's easy," he corrected himself, "but I can't treat him like a kid. The problem was that Jan finished his season in September, and then he likes to eat and he likes to live like everybody else for two months every winter. In those two months, he likes to get rid of his stress.

Jan Ullrich relaxing during the 1997 season. One of the big favorites for the 1998 Tour, he had to work hard early in the season to lose the weight he had gained during the winter and recapture his form.

"The winter before, he gained 10 kilos, but nobody saw it because he had no illness at the beginning of the season," and could race the weight off. But in 1998, "three times he had to fight a bad illness: once with his ear and two times bronchitis. So he had to interrupt his schedule and couldn't lose his kilos like the winter before. Not to worry," Pevenage said. "He'll be ready for the Tour. His form is coming."

Confirming that, Ullrich rode a good Classique des Alpes. On the third of seven climbs, the race exploded. As the first attack developed, who was that but Ullrich leading the pack in chase up the long ascent? Wearing his jersey of the German national champion, he looked as comfortable as he did when he was finishing second and then first in his first two Tours de France.

By the finish of the 181-kilometer race in Aix les Bains, only 47 riders of the 136-man field were left. Jalabert won in a sprint, beating Francesco Casagrande and Benoit Salmon. Ullrich was in the main chasing group behind the three leaders. He finished 14th in the same time as nine others, 1:44 behind, and looked strong.

The next day he left to reconnoiter some of the nearby alpine climbs that the Tour de France would pass over late in July. As he said in a rare public comment a few weeks before, "I'm more and more optimistic about the only day that counts for me—the start of the Tour."

15. Looking for Another Big One

NOBODY should ask Bjarne Riis if 1998 was a comeback year, because, as far as he was concerned, he hadn't been away. "No, really not," he says curtly. "Really not."

He knows as well as anybody that after he won the 1996 Tour de France convincingly, he finished seventh the next year, more than 18 minutes behind. He knows that among his five victories in 1997, the only one that mattered was in the Amstel Gold Classic in May, when he overpowered the field, rode alone to victory and indicated that his form for the Tour in July would be as dominant as it was the year before. Then he encountered the Tour's mountains and found that he suddenly could not climb them with the power and ease that he had shown in such abundance before.

And don't ask him if he was looking for revenge, because, the Danish rider insisted, he was not mad at anybody or anything. "The same," he says, "really not." He turned 34 in April 1998, old for a racer, but who can take revenge on time? The man who won the Tour de France the year before was Jan Ullrich, a decade younger than Riis. Who can take revenge on a teammate and friend?

So, no comeback and no revenge in 1998. Perhaps he hoped to prove something in the Tour de France?

"Might be," he responded with his first show of animation. "But really I don't think I have to prove anything," he said, lapsing. "What do I have to prove?"

He indulged in a long pause. The interview was going like a soliloquy from that other Dane, Prince Hamlet. "What do I have to prove?" he repeated. "To everybody and myself that I'm still going strong." He looked reassured by his answer.

Riis was eager, perhaps frantic, to show that he was not what some suspected: a one-off, a rider who won only one big race in a career that was then in its 12th year. A longtime support rider and lieutenant for stars, he became a star himself at his first opportunity, at 32. But the question remained, was he star or meteor?

Like Ullrich, Riis was behind in his schedule. He crashed during a training ride in Denmark in February and broke his right wrist, which kept him out of races for nearly two months.

Although the wrist still bothered him in April, and made it difficult to pull the handlebars, he said as he prepared for the one-day Classique des Alpes that he felt no discomfort. A stickler for diet and conditioning, he looked trim.

"I don't think I'm behind in my training," he said. He finished the multi-day Peace Race in May in fifth place—"Pretty good, yeah," he decided. "And last week I won a race in Spain," he added, referring to a stage in the Bicicleta Vasca. "No worries," he summed up, looking worried. That may be no more than the realization that the ball was over and Riis had turned back into a pumpkin.

When he left the Gewiss team in Italy at the end of the 1995 season and joined Telekom as a leader for the first time, he announced that his goal was to win the Tour de France, in which he had been fifth and third in two of the previous three years.

Telekom was a minor team when he joined it and in 1995 was allowed into the Tour only as a merged entry with the equally undistinguished ZG team from Italy. From the start, Riis instructed the team in diet (bee pollen is one of his secrets), training methods, and Thinking to Win.

"He's the one who took Telekom to this level," said teammate Udo Bolts. The emergence of Ullrich two years before, and the development of Erik Zabel as a star sprinter at the same time, contributed to the resurgence.

"Riis brought us a winning spirit," said Rudy Pevenage. "He's a real professional, always looking at the details. The other guys look to him and do what he's doing."

The Dane is famous for his careful preparation of a major race, scouting routes long beforehand and deciding where attacks are likely to succeed. In team meetings the day before a Tour de France stage, Riis will sometimes correct team officials who have mistakenly explained a bend in the road.

"They'll say it turns sharp to the right here and very politely Riis will say, 'No, it turns to the left there, they made a change over the winter,'" says somebody who knows about these team meetings.

Like Ullrich, who finished 14th, Riis rode a strong Classique des Alpes, finishing seventh, a second ahead of his teammate and rival in the Tour de France. Like Ullrich again, he left the next day to scout out sites in the Tour.

Ullrich was off to see most of the roads in the Alps, but Riis, who had already visited and ridden over these climbs that spring, was heading toward the only stretch he did not yet know, the 53 kilometers between Montceau les Mines and Le Creusot, where the final time trial was to be held a day before the finish in Paris. Often, that final time trial decides the race.

16. Champion for an Hour

THE CHAMPION's bouquet of spring flowers sat in the front of the team car. George Jean-Marie, the champion for not even an hour and a half, sat in the back, trying not to cry.

"They can't do this," he said. "They can't do this," he repeated, again and again.

Hincapie, 23 years old then and a leader of the U.S. Postal Service team, had just been stripped of the title of American professional champion, which he won earlier that Sunday in June 1997 in the CoreState USPRO Championship race in Philadelphia.

Officials ruled that, after the rear wheel of his bicycle went flat and was repaired with less than 10 miles (16 kilometers) to go in the 156-mile race, Hincapie was illegally paced back to the front group of riders by his team car. The penalty was to void the national championship he won by being the first American to finish the race.

"After his flat, he rode behind his team vehicle an excessive amount of time, more than two minutes," said Shawn Farrell, the head international official for the race. "I've never heard of a case where somebody motor-paced that long, that far, in front of so many people."

Mark Gorski, general manager of the U.S. Postal Service team, disputed Farrell on several counts. "We paced him into the caravan, which we have the right to do," said Gorski, who rode in his team car. "We were in front of him for 15 or 20 seconds. On the second warning, we pulled over."

Gorski, a gold medal sprinter at the 1984 Olympic Games, argued that the commissaires should have penalized the driver of the car, not Hincapie, for any infraction. The team planned to protest the decision to the sport's rulers, the International Cycling Union in Switzerland, Gorski said, not sounding optimistic.

Veteran observers of the sport could not recall a precedent for the disqualification. "Riders have been put out of a race for holding onto a team car and getting a tow," said Paul Sherwen, a former Tour de France rider who was an official for the championship's organizers. "But I've never heard of a rider who was disqualified for being motorpaced."

Gorski also questioned the 80 minutes it took the three commissaires to make their decision. During that time, Hincapie mounted the victory podium, received his flowers and his jersey, acknowledged proudly that his parents had come from New York City to watch him, and then attended a news conference.

"Tremendous, tremendous," he said immediately after he finished. "I've worked for this in this race for the last four years." His highest previous placing in the U.S. championship was 10th in 1995.

He would have succeeded his teammate Eddy Gragus in the red, white, and blue jersey. Instead it went to Bart Bowen, a rider for the Saturn team, who was also U.S. champion in 1992.

Hincapie said he had two flats during the long race in ideal weather, with just enough of a breeze to offset heat in the low 80s. The first flat occurred about halfway through and the second with two laps left.

"A really bad moment," he said. "I thought of all the bad luck I've had in races in Europe and thought, 'Not again.' But I got repaired quickly and my teammates helped and I rode hard to get back with the front group.

The American champion George Hincapie would move on to big things in the Tour. Here he is shown winning the sprint for third place in stage 3, bringing him to within 2 seconds from the yellow jersey.

"I've looked at so many riders in Europe wearing national champions' jerseys and thought, 'I want to be that.'"

Later, when he was sitting in his team car after he was told about his disqualification, Hincapie said he would not return the jersey he was wearing. He did not speak defiantly. He was shattered.

Trying to console him, a friend pointed out that he would not turn 24 until late that month. He had many more championships ahead of him, many more chances to win, the friend said.

Hincapie brushed the words away. "This was the year," he said. "They can't do this." He ducked his head then and covered his eyes with his hands.

The winner of the race was an Italian, Massimiliano Lelli of the Saeco-Cannondale team, who was ineligible for the U.S. national championship.

He crested the major climb in the CoreStates Championship for the last of ten times with a broad and surprised smile on his face. Not often thought of in European races as a dominating climber, Lelli was first over the top, and the smile meant that he realized he could win the race.

There still was a way to go, about 16 miles, but Lelli was right to smile. He easily won the race and its $25,000 first prize. Blowing kisses to the huge crowd, he finished the 156-mile journey in 5 hours 54 minutes 50 seconds, or 11 seconds ahead of Scott McGrory, an Australian with Die Continentale from Germany, and Hincapie.

When the standings were revised, Angel Canzonieri of the Saeco team was moved from fourth to third place and Bowen, who had finished eighth and the second American, was in the star-spangled jersey.

They say there are no happy endings? A year later, as his parents again watched, Hincapie won the race and the U.S. championship, surging across the finish line with his arms out. This time he kept the jersey and wore it proudly in the 1998 Tour de France.

PART II:

THE
TORTURED
TOUR

17. Mario the Magnificent

MARIO CIPOLLINI, the biggest hot dog outside the dreams of Oscar Mayer, came to Ireland for the start of the 1998 Tour de France with a bicycle as green as a shamrock.

The star Italian sprinter and showman arrived with his Saeco-Cannondale teammates and the 20 other teams of 9 men each in the three-week race. The riders began showing up for cursory medical examinations at Dublin Castle, and few were likely to attract more attention than Cipollini. Ireland is pretty fair bicycle racing territory and his exploits, including four daily stage victories in the recent Giro d'Italia, appeared to be well known in Dublin.

Cipollini has no Gaelic and less English, so would be spared explaining to the natives that his bicycle was not painted in honor of the Emerald Isle. Like his yellow bicycle, it was painted in honor of Cipollini.

He flaunted the yellow bicycle in 1997 during the four days that he wore the yellow jersey of the Tour's leader. Now, he said, his eye was on the green jersey of the points leader, hence the green bicycle.

A notoriously feeble climber, Cipollini would not need a bicycle with the red polka dots that denote the king of the mountains. But, as befits a clotheshorse who boasts that he has a pair of shoes for every day of the year, he did have in his Tour suitcase the same red, white, and blue, star-spangled outfit that he wore the year before to honor the American makers of his Cannondale bicycles and the black-and-blue-striped soccer jersey of Inter Milan with the No. 10 of Ronaldo that he wore on a victory podium in the Giro that May.

He and his team are fined every time he appears in anything but his regulation team jersey and black shorts but, hey, life's meant to be fun, Cipo says.

For all his sartorial bluster, his pet cheetah and Via Veneto scruffy good looks, the 31-year-old Cipollini is surprisingly soft-spoken. He does not predict victories and never humiliates his rivals verbally. While he may refer to himself as The Lion King, Il Magnifico, and even, a few years back, unblushingly as the Italian Stallion, he does not say he is the best sprinter in the sport. He agrees, however, with anybody who does say so.

"It's not easy being among the best for 10 years," he said during the Giro, where he tied Eddy Merckx's career record of 25 stage victories. "It's more difficult every year for me to train, to suffer. My biggest boost is that I win, which makes it worthwhile. I still feel an indescribable joy when I do. There's nothing like winning."

And he keeps winning. After his triumphs in the Giro, he went to Spain and won four stages in the Tour of Catalonia, his tune-up for the Tour de France.

His overall strategy in the Tour was the same as the year before: finish high in the short prologue and then try to win the first road race around Dublin or the second stage to Cork, gaining enough bonus seconds for victory to don the yellow jersey again and wear it to France. For the first week, the Tour's terrain would be flat—ideal for sprinters.

As always, Cipollini would rely on his Saeco teammates to overtake any breakaways and power him to the front near the mass finish. Saving energy, he would tuck in behind his leadout man, Gian Mateo Fagnini—a good enough sprinter himself to have won two stages in the last Giro—and then burst past him, and presumably everybody else, with 100 or 150 meters left.

Any sprint finish in the top 25 of the 189-man field would also give him the points, on a sliding scale of 35 down to one, that count toward the green jersey. That was Cipollini's main goal, he insisted, but to win the jersey, not just keep it for a few days, he would have to get over the Pyrenees and the Alps and make it to Paris.

It would not be simple. In his four previous Tours, citing the heat, lack of motivation, and general weariness, he was unable to finish. "They say I can't do it," he said, "but I think I can. When I get something in my head, I go for it."

18. On a Roller Coaster

THE WHOLE year had been a roller coaster ride, physically and mentally, for Chris Boardman, and now, as his biggest moment in the bicycle racing season arrived, he was speeding down, down, down.

"There's been things going on in my life that had influence on the sport," he said suddenly in Dublin. "Real life has interfered, and I'm not in the best shape I could be in. I'm afraid I'm not going to expand any more than that," he continued, even though he had not been pressed. "It's a personal matter."

With the Tour de France starting the next day, Boardman characterized his state of mind in one word: "depression." That was an extraordinary admission by the rider who had won the short opening prologue twice in the previous four years and who was the overwhelming favorite again when the 85th Tour began through the heart of Dublin.

"It's the world prologue championship," the 30-year-old Englishman said. "You've got to push. But," he continued, "my form is not there. Last year I came to the start and I thought, 'If all goes well, I should win. I might lose, but I should win.'" He did. "This year I'll probably be in the first five, and I might win. It's that way around.

"I'm not being negative," he insisted, "just realistic. That's the way it is this year. You don't always have the form that you want when you want it. This year, for various reasons, it's like that for me. But I'll just give it 110 percent and hope that's enough." Cordial and articulate as always, he neither looked nor sounded mournful.

Boardman, the leader of the Gan team, based in France, was troubled earlier in the season by what were described as gastric upsets. Partly in compensation for lost time, partly because he is addicted to training, he continued to work when many felt he should be slacking off a bit. The result was that he became overtrained and stale.

Worse, he began to overthink. By the time of the Prutour in England late in May, he had not yet won a race. "I'm riding below par, and as to why, I just do not know," he admitted there. "I've analyzed it. The evidence has been pulled apart many times. We still haven't come up with anything. It's quite scary but you get used to failure. You realize that you may very well be on a plateau, or even on the descent, but that's one of those things you don't want to talk about. You don't know where the top is until you're looking back at it. There is no peak until you start down the other side. For myself, it becomes a whole lot less interesting when you hit that plateau."

Boardman won the prologue in the Prutour and the first daily stage after that, finishing second overall when the week-long race reached London. Two weeks later, he won both the prologue and the long time trial in the Dauphiné Libéré race in France.

The Tour of Catelonia at the end of June went just as well, as he again won the prologue and the long time trial. Finally Boardman seemed to be on track.

In the two weeks before the Tour, however, he began to lose his power to recover, which is essential for a rider in a three-week race. In a newspaper column in England under his byline the previous week, he revealed that his four-year-old son Oscar had a higher level of testosterone, the male hormone, than he himself had.

While Boardman has never been able to cope with the race's high mountains, he might have been expected to be a major factor in the first long time trial, scheduled before the Pyrenees were entered. The course covered 58 kilometers (36 miles), a bit more than the 56.3 kilometers he traveled when he set the world record for the hour's ride against the clock in 1996.

Now his chances seemed doubtful, considering his pessimism about the prologue, his specialty. Boardman said he felt no special affinity for the Tour's start in Ireland, an English-speaking country where people drive on the left, the food is at best hearty, and the weather is cool, rainy, and overcast—all like home in Liverpool.

"It's no different," he said, "the Tour de France is the Tour de France, wherever it may start. I feel under tremendous pressure because I feel the responsibility that I have with the team. This is what I'm paid to do. But when things haven't gone well in the buildup, the security isn't there and it's not a very pleasant time in the waiting game, waiting for it to happen."

19. The Festina Case: Part One

EVEN before the Tour de France began in Dublin, officials were scrambling to explain a drug scandal involving one of the major teams in the race.

The facts were few: Willy Voet, a Belgian soigneur for the Festina team, which is based in France, had been arrested at the French-Belgian border when his car—an official Tour car bearing the team insignia—was found to be carrying a large quantity of such banned drugs as steroids and the artificial hormone EPO. Although the arrest was made on July 8, it was not revealed until late July 10, a day before the start.

Bruno Roussel, the directeur sportif of Festina, insisted at a news conference hours before the prologue that the soigneur had not been part of his crew at the Tour. "Let the French police do their work and find out what's going on," he said. "We know nothing about this. End of statement."

Jean-Marie Leblanc, director of the Tour de France, was equally terse. "If it is a doping case," he said, "it's not directly connected to a rider and not directly connected to this race. It happened hundreds of kilometers from here."

He added that there was no question of disqualifying the Festina riders or making any judgment until more facts were known. That was unlikely to happen for a few days, or until the race reached France, when Tour officials could confer with the police there.

20. On the Sidelines

PLUMP, stately Stephen Roche was one of the major spokesmen for the start of the Tour de France in Ireland, as befitted the native of Dublin who won the race in 1987 and whose photograph, in full racing gear, hangs everywhere in the city years after his retirement.

Sean Kelly, who rode in 14 Tours and won the green points jersey four times, was also honored in Dublin, but nowhere near as much as he would be when the race passed into County Tipperary and his home town of Carrick on Suir.

The late Shay Elliott, a pioneer Irishman in professional bicycle racing and the holder of the Tour's yellow jersey for three days in 1963, was similarly celebrated, as was Martin Earley, a clever, hard-working team rider and the winner of a Tour stage a decade previously.

In the publicity buildup for the Tour, none of Ireland's handful of retired riders who rode the race more than once seemed to have been forgotten—except for Paul Kimmage. His name appeared nowhere except in the *Sunday Independent*, the newspaper he writes for, and on the book that had just been reissued eight years after it scandalized many people in the world of professional bicycle racing. It also sold 15,000 copies, which he calls "pretty good for a sports book," and won an award in Britain as the sports book of 1990.

Titled *A Rough Ride*, it tells how Kimmage and some other riders used drugs—mainly amphetamine stimulants and steroids—to be competitive. "I was never a cheat," he wrote. "I WAS A VICTIM," he insisted in capital letters.

"My perception at the time was that we were victims of a corrupt system," he said in an interview before the race began. Kimmage did not feel that the system had improved since he retired in 1989 during the Tour de France, the third he rode in his four-year professional career.

"The drugs problem has changed," he said. "It's moved on from amphetamines and steroids to EPO," which multiplies the red blood corpuscles that carry oxygen to muscles and which, because it thickens the blood, is suspected in a handful of rider deaths attributed to heart attacks.

"That's a bad change, a very bad change. It's a change that happened due to earlier neglect by the authorities," notably the International Cycling Union, which governs the sport. "This attitude of sweeping it under the carpet, the law of silence, has done a lot of damage to the sport. I think they're paying for it now."

So was the 36-year-old Kimmage, in his way. "I haven't been treated very kindly in the run-up to this race," he said. "If I wasn't working as a journalist, I wouldn't be here now—I'd be on the other side of the barriers. I believe that very strongly. I'd be lying if I said it didn't sadden me, didn't disappoint me hugely.

"To be fair, when they list Stephen and Sean and Shay and Martin, they've won stages in the Tour and written their names in the legends. But I do believe there's an underlying current of 'This guy's written a book that we didn't like, and now we're going to make him pay for it; we're not going to let him forget it when the Tour comes to Ireland.'

"I love the sport," he continued. "It was from love of the sport that I took the decision to write the book. Because it would have been easy to take a new job on the paper, say nothing, and be buddy-buddy and pally-wally with everyone. But what sort of service would I have done to the kids who were coming into the game?

"The attitude is 'You cannot be anti-drug and pro-sport.' I'm totally pro-sport. They perceive that if you talk about drugs, you do damage to the sport, which is absolute, complete nonsense."

Roche disagrees. He and Kimmage were more than friends before the book, which is full of flattering—Kimmage now calls them "fawning"—references to the rider who in 1987 won the Tour, the Giro d'Italia, and the world championship road race in the same year. They were the tribute paid to a star by an admitted domestique, or servant, a rider whose finest result was a sixth place in the amateur world championship. "As a pro cyclist, I was Mr. Bloody Average," Kimmage wrote in his book.

"I don't know what's up with Paul," Roche said in another interview. "Paul wrote his book, and I was stung by it. We talked a couple of times, and I told him I didn't like it.

"No, we haven't been reconciled. He has to wake up some time and realize what he's doing to the sport in general. Yes, it's OK to wake everybody up to the danger of drugs, I do agree, but at the same time there's a limit as to what you can say. He's said it once, OK, but he keeps saying it again.

"I say kids today need sport to keep them out of trouble, to keep them away from drugs, to keep them out of delinquence. So encourage them to ride a bike. Don't tell them that if you want to ride a bike well, you have to take drugs. Say it a little but don't go on and on, please."

To which Kimmage would reply: "The book was written to highlight the ambivalence of the authorities to the problem. They were the target. It wasn't the bike riders. The book wasn't written to portray those who do drugs as baddies and those who don't as goodies.

"Once the system addresses the problem and the guys keep taking stuff, they're no longer victims. That's when they become cheats. When the preventive measures are in place, and the penalties are laid down, and they still insist on looking for the edge, then they become cheats.

"But the authorities haven't answered to the problem," Kimmage said, his face darkening even before he knew of the Festina scandal. "They have to, they can't keep ignoring it."

21. The Prologue

WHATEVER was troubling Chris Boardman obviously cleared up overnight as he opened the 85th Tour with an easy victory in the short prologue.

"I'm surprised," he said moments before he donned the yellow jersey of the leader of the race. For the previous 24 hours, he had been complaining about his lack of form, his "depression," and unspecified personal problems that he said were interfering with his performance. He also won the Tour's prologues in 1994 and 1997.

"I was at my best," the Briton explained simply. "And I was lucky with the weather."

What a foreigner considered an intermittent sprinkle, but what the Irish regard as an integral part of the air, like oxygen, ended early in the afternoon, a couple of hours before Boardman set off in the 189-man field. The roads were mainly dry for his run of 6 minutes 12 seconds 36 hundredths of a second over the 5.6-kilometer (3.5-mile) course.

That was four seconds better than the Spaniard Abraham Olano with the Banesto team, who was regarded as much more of an overall favorite in the Tour than Boardman. Olano would be far stronger in the many mountains that fill the Tour's course.

Third, five seconds back, was Laurent Jalabert, the leader of the ONCE team from Spain, the French national champion, and the world champion in the time trial. The prologue, in effect, is a time trial, and the riders set off a minute apart.

Fourth, also five seconds behind in a splendid performance, was an American, Bobby Julich. Julich is a strong rider in long time trials, not usually in short ones, like the prologue.

He is also a fine climber who finished 17th overall in the last Tour, his first, and said before his start in Dublin that his sights were set higher this year. "Last year I didn't know what to expect and this year I do," he said.

Fifth was Christophe Moreau, a Frenchman with Festina who was appearing in the Tour while his appeal from a positive drug finding in a spring race was being weighed. Jan Ullrich, the German leader of the

Telekom team, who won the last Tour and then struggled with his weight all spring, showed that he was back in condition by finishing sixth, five seconds behind the winner.

The crowds all along the way, from the start at Trinity College through the swank section called Georgian Dublin, into the rundown Liberties and across the River Liffey, were big at the beginning of the three-hour exercise, although they thinned out near the end.

Why was the start held in Dublin? Why not? The Tour had started abroad twice in the past few years, in the Netherlands in 1996 and in Spain in 1992, if never across a body of water from France. The big reason this time was to avoid media and fan competition at home from the soccer World Cup; to keep the overlap to a minimum, the bicycle race started a week later than usual, holding its prologue and first stage as the World Cup was staging its third-place and championship games. By the time the Tour reached the motherland, the reasoning went, the World Cup would be just a memory.

The Tour's start had been controversial among the Irish in a small way. While such retired Irish stars as Stephen Roche and Sean Kelly proclaimed it "a major event for Dublin and an even bigger event for Ireland in view of tourism," as Roche put it, some merchants were unhappy.

Dublin is a city of motorists, and O'Connell Street, a main shopping area and the site of the prologue's finish and the start of the first stage, had been closed to traffic for two days. Closed too for the prologue day were many other streets, causing the chamber of commerce to warn that millions of dollars in trade would be lost during the weekend.

To the merchants, that seemed a heavy cost in addition to the $3 million that the Irish government paid to stage the beginning of the race.

Nevertheless, O'Connell Street began filling with spectators by midmorning, five hours before the prologue, and the crowds were deep against the barriers by noon. As they awaited the riders, thousands of spectators made frequent forays into the souvenir shops and fast-food emporiums that line the street.

A favorite spot to watch was in front of the General Post Office, the site in 1916 of the Easter Uprising that led to a weeklong siege and eventual independence from Britain. The premises were marked not only by a plaque bearing the stirring words, "We declare the right of the people of Ireland to the ownership of Ireland and to the unfettered control of Irish destinies," but also by a Tour de France sign advising the riders that they had 100 meters to go to the finish line.

"Le Grand Départ," as the Irish were calling the opening of the Tour, was off to a fine, international start.

22. Stage One: Steels Starts His Collection

THE LEADING players were the same, but this time Erik Zabel did not swerve and have to be penalized, and Tom Steels did not throw his water bottle at Frédéric Moncassin and have to be ejected although, once again, Moncassin, of the Gan team, did do his best to win—to no avail.

In a replay of a celebrated sprint finish early in the previous Tour de France, Steels, the Belgian national champion, was on his best behavior in the first stage, and that was enough to give him a victory–the first of four he'd collect before this Tour would end.

At the end of a 180.5-kilometer (112-mile) ride in and around chilly Dublin, Steels, who works for the Mapei team, easily beat Zabel, the German national champion and a member of the Telekom team. Robbie McEwen, an Australian with Rabobank, was third and Moncassin was sixth.

The winner was timed in 4 hours 29 minutes 58 seconds, a speed of 40 kilometers an hour despite strong headwinds in a countryside made more verdant as a thin mist turned occasionally to drizzle.

Continuing by four seconds in the overall leader's yellow jersey was Chris Boardman, who after he had overcome his doubts and despair to win the prologue, was just as dubious about his chances to keep the jersey after the first of 21 stages. He said that he expected a sprinter to gain enough bonus seconds with a victory to take the jersey.

The obvious choice was Mario Cipollini, who finished just 13 seconds behind Boardman in the prologue. But Cipollini crashed, with about half a dozen other riders, eight kilometers from the finish in Phoenix Park.

He was not injured but lost 3 minutes 40 seconds before he could get back in the chase. The fall was caused by a teammate's inattention and a brushed wheel on a wide section of the road, not the usual nervousness among the 189 riders in the early stages of the three-week race.

Crowds were huge all along the route, which stretched south to Arklow on the coast before heading back to the capital through the Wicklow Mountains.

As they were during the prologue, the police were out in force, with 3,000 officers working on crowd control and anti-terrorist activities. The organizers of the historic start in Dublin were keeping a wary eye on the sectarian standoff in Northern Ireland and hoping it did not spill over into a disruption of the Tour, similar to the ones that farmers, steelworkers, and dockyard workers have staged in France in the past. It was an Irishman, James Joyce, after all, who wrote, "History is a nightmare from which I am trying to awake."

23. Stage Two: King Kelly Day

WHAT started as a festival day in the Tour de France to celebrate a hero of the past, Sean Kelly, ended in disaster for a hero of the present, Chris Boardman, the man in the leader's yellow jersey.

Boardman was injured and taken off on a stretcher after he seemed to brush the back wheel of teammate Frédéric Moncassin and crashed, sliding along the shoulder of a wide highway and into a stone wall.

He lay immobile on his back until the race's ambulance quickly arrived. Dr. Gérard Porte, the Tour's chief medical officer, said at first that Boardman appeared to have a broken bone in his temple but was otherwise uninjured. At an Irish hospital, he was found to have broken his collarbone but only bruised his temple. After being kept overnight for observation because he struck his helmeted head in the fall and was unconscious for a few minutes, he left for home in England.

This was the second time Boardman has been injured and forced to withdraw from the Tour. In 1995, he crashed as he took a curve in the rain during the opening prologue and broke his ankle.

Crashes are common in the Tour, especially in the early, nervous stages. Another crash in the first stage decked Laurent Jalabert, Laurent Brochard, the Frenchman who was the world road race champion, and Abraham Olano. All were quickly up and back riding.

In 1995, Jalabert lost the yellow jersey early on when he was delayed as part of a mass collision and in 1991, the Danish rider Rolf Sorensen was unable to start the next day after he broke a collarbone in a crash while he was the early race leader.

The race always continues, of course. An hour after the crash, and 5 hours 45 minutes and 10 seconds after the pack set off in cordial Enniscorthy, where long lines of costumed people stood with high pikes to signify their Viking ancestry on the 205.5-kilometer (127.5-mile) run to Cork, Jan Svorada, a Czech with the Mapei team, won a mass sprint by a bicycle length.

Second was Robbie McEwen, who was obviously in splendid form, since he was third in the sprint the day before. Third in the field of 186 men was Mario Cipollini, who lost nearly four minutes in the first stage after he and several other riders crashed.

Moving into the vacated yellow jersey because of time bonuses along the route was the German Telekom rider Erik Zabel. Second was another sprinter, Tom Steels, and third was Moncassin.

In addition to the loss of Boardman, the field dropped from its original 189 riders when Ludovic Auger of the Big Mat team did not start and Erik Dekker of Rabobank had to quit partway through because of injuries in the Cipollini crash.

Sean Kelly too had to pull out of the Tour once because of a crash, in 1987, that left him with a broken collarbone.

King Kelly he was then, winning every bicycle race in sight except the Tour de France, and King Kelly he remains now: This was unofficially Sean Kelly Day in the 85th Tour. Until Boardman's crash, it was, as they say in Ireland, brilliant.

Kelly, who retired four years before at the age of 38, rode in 14 Tours, and finished 12 of them. In addition to capturing the green points jersey a record four times, he won five daily stages and for a day, in 1983, wore the yellow jersey.

Irish fans rolled out the green carpet throughout the opening stages of the 1998 Tour while the race visited the Emerald Isle for the first time.

A farmer's son, he lives still in his home town of Carrick on Suir, which he said in an interview before the stage is "a strong cycling town. They call it the home of cycling in Ireland."

"They're very enthusiastic down there in the countryside," he said, "more so than in Dublin. They're decorating all the shop windows and there's a lot of flags and banners. They're really making a big thing about it. Of course, it's fabulous, a dream come true, that the Tour has come to Ireland."

Crowds were indeed huge and enthusiastic along the route despite a cold wind and occasional showers. French flags mingled with Irish ones, and posters acclaiming Kelly hung from many a pole and window.

Since 1985, a main area in Carrick on Suir, a village of 5,000, has been called Sean Kelly Square, and through there the pack streamed near noon as a crowd estimated at several times the population cheered.

Originally, the Tour was to have bypassed the square because the opening into it was considered too narrow for safety. "A tight part of the street," Kelly called it.

"They wanted to route the race just at the outskirts of town, and the people down there weren't too happy," he said. Local officials met with the Tour director, Jean-Marie Leblanc, to reason.

A one-ton limestone boulder, called a jostling stone, at the end of the square next to Jack Savage's butcher shop, was uprooted from the spot where it had rested since the 17th century. A few telephone poles were removed, the sidewalk cut back.

Finally, Kelly was standing on a podium to watch as the Tour passed through his square. An explosion of cheers rang out for all the riders and for King Kelly, then, now, and forever.

24. Le Tour à France

THE TOUR put the "de France" back into its name at Roscoff, ending the second Year of the French in Ireland much as the first one did exactly two centuries before: The visitors sailed off in the night. This time, though, they left behind happy memories.

In 1798, a small Napoleonic force was sent to aid an Irish uprising against the British and, when it began to fail, the French hoisted anchor and left the rebellion's leaders, notably Wolfe Tone, to face the consequences. They were grave, as the many Wolfe Tone squares, quays, and streets in Ireland attest.

The visit went much better this time. All along the routes of the prologue and the first two stages in Ireland, the French flag was flown with the Irish, and bilingual signs proclaimed "Bienvenue à Tipperary, Welcome to Tipperary" or wherever. Crowds of spectators were immense and the race's staging areas were awash in folk dancers, long ranks of friendly people with pikes to denote their Viking heritage, and plentiful food and drink.

After the second stage into Cork, the 186 remaining riders and their team officials were flown to Brittany. The 2,000 other members of the entourage and their many cars and trucks were put aboard three ferries to cross the Channel overnight. Just before sailing, an Irish bagpipe band on shore began serenading the visitors. Many Bretons are Celts too, and a French bagpipe band aboard one ferry took up the lament.

As the last strains of "The Minstrel Boy to the War Has Gone" was just dying, the ship pulled away from the slip. Ashore, the organizing committee for the Tour's visit released hundreds of balloons, some blue, some white and some red for the French colors.

The balloons were still rising as the ferry passed Cobh and began a slow turn starboard, away from Ireland and toward France.

25. Stage Three: Vain Hopes

EVERY French bicycle racer dreams of winning the big one—a stage of the Tour de France on July 14, the national holiday—and Xavier Jan came about as close as he could. Close was half the length of a bicycle, and it was good for just second place.

"I didn't have much luck," said the 28-year-old Frenchman, who rides for La Française des Jeux. "Yes," he agreed, "it would have wonderful on the Quatorze Juillet," July 14.

But this was the New Europe, the one with no national boundaries and a forthcoming universal currency. So the huge French crowd in Brittany sounded more or less sincere as they cheered the victory of a German, Jens Heppner of the Telekom team, instead of one of their own.

With a little more than a kilometer of the 169-kilometer (105-mile) third stage left, Heppner and Jan accelerated away from their partners in a long breakaway by nine men, three of them French. The two leaders played cat and mouse, watching each other until the final 150 meters, when Heppner jumped ahead and crossed the line first.

Third, two seconds behind, and at the head of the remaining six riders, was George Hincapie. He said afterward that he had cramped in his right thigh near the end. "I knew I could tough out a sprint, but I couldn't chase and catch those two and then sprint," he said. His highest finish in three Tours de France moved Hincapie, then 25 years old and the American national champion, into second place overall.

He was two seconds behind the new leader, Bo Hamburger, a Dane with Casino, who was also part of the nine-man breakaway and finished fourth. In third place overall was Stuart O'Grady, an Australian member of the Gan team, who finished fifth.

Heppner, 33, is a team worker for Telekom, usually in charge of shepherding Jan Ullrich. He joined the breakaway, which lasted 124 kilometers, as a routine protective measure for his team, guaranteeing that if the riders won by a big margin, a Telekom representative would be among them.

The attackers finished 1 minute 10 seconds ahead of the main pack as Heppner, who moved to fourth place overall, was timed in 3 hours 33 minutes 36 seconds in the southward run through Brittany from the port of Roscoff. And, since this was Brittany, the artichoke center of the western world, along the way the riders passed vast fields of the vegetable, which proved to grow on stalks, not, as some botanists supposed, in the earth like its cousin, the potato.

26. The Festina Case: Part Two

AS THE RACE reached Cholet, the Festina management, under increasing pressure in the drug scandal, announced that the head of the team was being questioned by the French police. Other reports said that he was in official custody, but not arrested, and would be held until his lawyer arrived.

Bruno Roussel, the directeur sportif of the nine Festina riders in the Tour de France, had been asking for two days, since the race came to France from its start in Ireland, for the inquiry so that he could answer

Despite the growing drug scandal surrounding the team, the Festina riders rode aggressively throughout the opening week. At the start of stage one they received medals as the top-placed team in the race.

"rumors," the management noted. Its announcement did not mention that the police had also searched the team's hotel in Cholet. Willy Voet, the jailed soigneur, after first insisting that all the drugs found in his car by the French police were for his personal use, was said to have admitted that he was taking them to Dublin for delivery to the team doctor under orders from Festina team officials.

Both Roussel and team doctor Eric Ryckaert denied this and Roussel announced the night before the police came for him that he had instructed his lawyer to act against publication of what he termed hearsay and rumors, violating his rights under French law.

But French newspapers continued to report leaks in the case, attributing them—if at all—to unidentified judicial sources. Newspapers also reported that the police searched the team's headquarters near Lyon and confiscated illegal drugs.

The sponsor of the team, Miguel Rodriguez, a Spanish watch manufacturer, said that if an intention to use illegal drugs was proven, he would immediately terminate his contract, which runs through 2001.

Tour officials noted that the arrest was made far from the race and before it began. When the affair became public before the start, Tour director Jean-Marie Leblanc ruled out any penalties until more facts became known.

He repeated that position in Cholet in a television appearance, saying that for now there was no question of ejecting the team, which included Laurent Brochard, the world road race champion, and two favorites in the Tour, Richard Virenque and Alex Zulle.

But Roger Legeay, the coach of the Gan team in the Tour and the head of the French league of professional cycling, said on the same program, "The Tour is supposed to be a festival. We can't have a festival with this hanging over us. This must be resolved quickly."

27. Stage Four: Doing Their Best

A FEW Americans' hearts were broken on a slight uphill on the D1 two-lane road at a spot marked by a green banner just outside the village of Plumelec in western France.

Foremost among those affected was George Hincapie, who wore the red, white, and blue star-spangled jersey of the U.S. national road race champion. "It's been a dream of mine to wear the jersey in the Tour de France especially," Hincapie said before the start of the daily stage. "The only thing I'd trade it for is the yellow jersey."

As he spoke, the U.S. Postal Service rider was second in the overall standings, two seconds behind the Tour's leader, the man in the yellow jersey. Hincapie, his teammates, and their officials knew that if he finished first, second, or third in the first of three time-bonus sprints during the day, and the leader, Bo Hamburger finished behind him, the American would be the race's virtual leader.

"I know it'll be hard, but you can't pass up a chance like this," said Hincapie. "I can hope. I feel confident, and I'm going to try my best. I'm a little nervous, excited, but that's the Tour de France."

This was Hincapie's third Tour. A teammate and another American, Frankie Andreu, had already ridden six editions of the world's greatest bicycle race and finished all of them. With that much more experience, he put the mission into perspective: "It'll be hard. The whole team will ride to put George in position to sprint, but it'll be a very difficult two seconds to come by."

In the end, it was too difficult.

Stuart O'Grady, the Australian who was in third place overall and a second behind Hincapie, won the sprint and the six bonus seconds deducted from his overall elapsed time. Hincapie was third, gaining two seconds that no longer mattered. O'Grady was now the virtual leader, as Hamburger gained no time.

The Australian, 24 and a member of the Olympic champion pursuit team, also won the second bonus sprint and finished third in the final one, while neither Hincapie nor Hamburger scored.

At the end of the fourth of 21 stages, a 252-kilometer (156-mile) journey from Plouay in Brittany to Cholet in the Loire region, O'Grady exchanged his virtual leadership for the real thing—he mounted the victory podium and slipped into the yellow jersey. "I don't know if it's the greatest day of my life," he said, "but I don't know how it can get any better. Ever since I began racing, I've dreamed of wearing the yellow jersey. It's mine—even if I have it for a minute."

He led Hamburger, in second place, by 11 seconds, with Hincapie third, also 11 seconds behind.

The flat stage was won in a sprint finish by Jeroen Blijlevens, a Dutchman with TVM, in a time of 5 hours 48 minutes 32 seconds, an average speed of 43 kilometers an hour in chilly weather. Second was Nicola Minali, an Italian with Riso Scotti, half a bicycle length behind, and third was the Czech Jan Svorada, the victor two days before.

O'Grady, Hamburger, and Hincapie all finished in a large bunch of riders 8 seconds behind the winner. The American was among a handful who were slowed by another mass crash, about 2 kilometers from the finish, but got up quickly and sped off. Another victim was Mario Cipollini, the world's top sprinter, who was unable to compete in his specialty for the second time in this 85th Tour because of a crash.

Hincapie was disappointed afterward, but not crushed. "I did my best," he said. "Not good enough."

Noting that the next day's stage also had three bonus sprints, a U.S. Postal Service team official, Dan Osipow, said, "We're not done yet. George is only 11 seconds back. We'll try to be just as aggressive tomorrow."

All nine riders on the team seemed keyed up as they awaited the start while thousands of spectators strolled among them, seeking autographs and a friendly word. Brittany is mad about bicycle racing, and Plouay, the start, is particularly wild about the sport and annually stages a one-day race that attracts many tens of thousands of spectators. The town will be the host to the world championships in 2000.

One of six Americans in the Tour, Hincapie did his share of posing for photographs. Like him, his teammates were guardedly optimistic.

"The team will do its best to get him up there at the front and then it's up to George," said Marty Celsius. "We all know it will be tough but we're hoping."

Two Americans on a rival team, Cofidis, were also rooting for George Hincapie.

"I think George has a great chance," said Kevin Livingston. They were teammates on Motorola two years ago. "He's a good friend, and I'd like to see it happen."

Bobby Julich, another former Motorola rider, agreed. "I was speaking to Kevin," he said, "and we think maybe this is the year an American takes the yellow jersey. No one has had it since Greg LeMond in 1991.

"It's such a big honor to represent America in this race, because cycling isn't so popular back home. It takes a lot of character to be in this sport, because when you're growing up, all your friends are playing baseball, football, and basketball, and you're doing an obscure sport called cycling.

"But it all becomes worth it when you ride in the Tour. That's the pinnacle of the sport. And the yellow jersey is the pinnacle of the pinnacle. I would love to see George in the yellow jersey."

As Osipow said, maybe the next day.

28. Stage Five: The Lion King Roars

THERE was another crash near the finish of a Tour stage but this time Mario Cipollini, Il Magnifico, was not in the middle of the sprawled bodies and bicycles as he had been twice that week.

Cipollini was way ahead of the accident—about two bicycle lengths ahead of everybody, in fact. He had plenty of time to raise his arms in his usual triumphal benediction and even to glance back as if he wondered where the rest of the 183-man pack was.

The Lion King (as he is called for his tawny, highlighted mane and regal air) registered his victory on the kind of terrain he likes best: an extremely long straightaway at the end of a flat 228.5-kilometer (142-mile) fifth stage from Cholet to Chateauroux in the heart of France.

"I've been waiting," he said of the earlier mishaps. "This was a perfect stage for me, and my teammates did everything right."

Saeco riders led the train into the grimy city and then left Cipollini to pour on the final coals himself. He easily finished ahead of Erik Zabel and Christophe Mengin, a Frenchman with La Française des Jeux, second and third among a swarm at the end of the milelong straightaway.

In one of those nice touches the Tour often provides, the finish line was placed outside the house of Marcel Dussault, who won three stages in the Tour more than 40 years before and briefly wore the yellow jersey in 1949 after capturing the first stage. Oldtimers say Dussault took the symbol of leadership by winning a sprint finish as easily as Cipollini did.

The Italian was timed in 5 hours 18 minutes 49 seconds, an average speed of 42 kilometers an hour, on a gloomy day with frequent chilly drizzles. Whatever happened to summer?

Cipollini entered the Tour after registering four sprint victories in the Giro d'Italia and four more in the Tour of Catalonia. He had time for another notch in his gun before the race reached the Pyrenees.

In the contest for overall leadership, Stuart O'Grady retained the yellow jersey as George Hincapie moved up a step to second place overall by finishing second in the first of three bonus time sprints to take four seconds off his total elapsed time. Hincapie trailed O'Grady by seven seconds, with Bo Hamburger in third place, 11 seconds behind.

As they did the day before, the U.S. Postal Service riders went all out to give Hincapie good position in the bonus sprints. After his second-place finish, he was trapped by a crash in the second sprint and, in the third, was unable to gain any of the 6-4-2 seconds awarded to the first three men across the line because they had been scooped up by a three-man breakaway.

Order was restored and the pack rode intact long before Chateauroux was reached. Hincapie did his best to win the final sprint but said, "The roads were slick from the rain and I kept worrying about crashes."

In the last dash, he was bumped by Zabel and Jaan Kirsipuu, an Estonian with Casino, and swerved to his left briefly and dangerously.

Kirsipuu and Silvio Martinello, an Italian with Polti, both crashed. Hincapie stayed upright and finished a strong seventh, though gaining no bonus time.

29. The Festina Case: Part Three

SEEKING to keep the burgeoning drug scandal from swamping the Tour de France, the international governing body of bicycle racing announced before the start of the fifth stage that it had suspended the coach of the Festina team after he was taken into police custody.

The coach, 41-year-old Frenchman Bruno Roussel, was accused by a team worker of ordering him to bring to the start of the Tour illegal performance-enhancing drugs, including amphetamines, steroids, masking drugs and the artificial hormone EPO, a chemical that multiplies the red blood corpuscles that carry oxygen to muscles.

EPO, which cannot be detected directly in the blood or urine, is suspected to be in wide use in such endurance sports as bicycle racing and cross-country skiing. Because it thickens the blood, it has been blamed in more than a dozen deaths by heart attacks among amateur and professional riders in recent years.

Endurance athletes tend to have a resting pulse in the 30s—less than half that of the man in the street—and blood thickened with EPO could coagulate abnormally at a low pulse rate, especially when a raider is sleeping, causing cardiac arrest, doctors say.

For two years, officials had made spot checks of riders' levels of red blood cells, suspending for two weeks anybody whose level was above 50 percent. Nearly a dozen riders were penalized in 1997 and about half a dozen by the time the Tour started in July.

Roussel was held after a few hours of questioning in the town of Cholet. Also being held was the team's doctor, Eric Ryckaert, 52, a Belgian. They were not formally arrested or charged but could be held for 96 hours and were scheduled to be transferred to the northern city of Lille, where the drug case was being investigated, for further questioning.

"This affair has shaken the confidence of the public and disturbed the riders," said Tour director Jean-Marie Leblanc at a news conference as the suspension was announced. "We hope that from this moment, sport will return to its rightful priority in the Tour."

At his side was Martin Bruin, the race's chief commissaire, or judge, representing the International Cycling Union, which suspended Roussel's license "provisionally."

"That means for the time being," Bruin explained in a preview of the announcement. "Other than that, the official comment is that there is no comment."

The International Cycling Union, which is universally known as the UCI from its initials in French, the language of professional cycling, cited Roussel's failure to respond in writing to questions it raised.

Those questions concerned the arrest a week before of Willy Voet, 53, a Festina soigneur—a masseur, a gopher, a confidant of the riders, and often their unofficial doctor. He had first told the French police that the drugs were for his personal use and then that he was taking them, under team orders, to the Festina doctor in Dublin, where the Tour began.

Roussel and Dr. Ryckaert both denied Voet's accusation. Nevertheless, a drawn Leblanc said, "There are sufficiently grave conditions" to suspend Roussel's license. He might have been referring to coverage by French newspapers, which universally featured the drug case on their front pages and relegated the race results to inside pages.

Leblanc was a professional rider himself at the time of the Tour's biggest drug affair, the death in 1967 of the British rider Tom Simpson during a climb on Mont Ventoux. Amphetamines were blamed when Simpson overheated during the stage and suffered a fatal heart attack.

The Tour's last major doping scandal occurred in 1988, when the race leader, the Spaniard Pedro Delgado, failed a drug test because he had used a masking agent for steroids. Delgado was allowed to continue to triumph in Paris because the drug was illegal under most standards but not for a few more weeks under those of the UCI. Leblanc, by then a journalist, took over command of the race the next year.

Four riders—usually the stage winner, the man in the yellow jersey, and two men chosen at random—are tested for drugs each day in the Tour. There has been only one announced failure in the 1990s.

The Tour director said that he had talked by phone with Hein Verbruggen, the head of the UCI, which was meeting in Havana, and that Verbruggen had been "disturbed by press coverage of the affair and the image it is giving to the Tour."

As for the nine Festina riders in the race, Leblanc repeated his stand that "Nothing has been proved against them," and that therefore they were not subject to expulsion or any other penalty.

Bruin also said that the riders faced no immediate sanctions. "Again for the time being, it has nothing to do with the riders. It has everything to do with the soigneur and some details that have come to the attention of the UCI executive committee." He would not specify the details.

The suspension, announced in Cholet as a cold drizzle fell on officials, riders, and journalists before the start of the stage, was controversial.

"I don't think it's fair," said Patrick Lefévère, the directeur sportif of the Mapei team, which was ranked No. 2, just below Festina, in the computerized standings. "Until a person is found guilty, he's innocent. 'Provisional suspension,' bah. If after this he's found not guilty, is the UCI going to pay him for damage to his reputation? I don't think so.

"If he ordered the soigneur to do this, he's guilty," Lefévère continued in an interview. "But if the soigneur was trafficking in drugs and the directeur sportif didn't know about it, he's not guilty. And in that case there's a lot of damage for nothing."

Bernard Thévénet, twice winner of the Tour in the 1970s and now a television commentator, put it this way: "It's a very delicate matter. What's the right way to go? That's the problem. Is this enough to lift the cloud over the race? But at least the UCI has tried to do something."

Johnny Weltz, directeur sportif of the U.S. Postal Service team, said, "It's hard to figure out what's the real story. He has his legal rights but the UCI may know something we don't, and that's why they acted."

Festina riders were supportive of Roussel and somewhat defiant. Richard Virenque, who was among the favorites, said at a news conference, "We're here to win the Tour de France, and we'll continue to ride to do so. We're not here to discuss doping. I'll answer questions about the stage today but not about this affair."

Neil Stephens, an Australian with Festina, was more forthcoming. "The team is pretty depressed," he said in an interview. "We've got a couple of mates involved in pretty heavy stuff, and we're just trying to get on with it."

Referring to Roussel, he added: "Bruno said a couple of days ago he wanted to go to the court, he wanted to talk. He said he's got nothing to hide, he wanted to get everything out of the way. He said to me yesterday morning, 'One of these days the coppers are going to come for me and take me away'—he was quite willing to talk. We're going to let justice do its bit and we're going to do our bit and try to win the Tour de France. So let's get on with it."

30. Stage Six: A Lesson in Team Tactics

COME along for a ride at the front of the Tour de France. There are three riders in a breakaway, 6 minutes 30 seconds ahead of the rest of the 181-man field: Max Sciandri, the dual-nationality Italian-Briton who rides for La Française des Jeux; the Frenchman Cédric Vasseur, who rides for Gan, and José Rodriguez, a Spaniard with Kelme. They are riding in single file, working together by taking a turn at the front as the two others ride in the slipstream during the 204.5-kilometer (127-mile) sixth stage.

With 50 kilometers to go, their coaches, who are close behind in cars, all doubt that the riders can hold off the pack. If they do, two of the three coaches are pessimistic about their man's chances in a final sprint.

"They've got a 30 percent chance of staying away," says Serge Beucherie, the assistant directeur sportif of the Gan team, as he leans out the window, still steering, and chats with a reporter in another car. "The rest are beginning to come up awfully fast." He rates Vasseur's chances of winning a sprint as none.

In another team car, Yvon Madiot, the assistant directeur sportif of La Française des Jeux, also rates the overall chance of success at 30 percent. "If they last," he says, "Sciandri has a 50 percent chance of beating the Gan."

José Ignacio Labarta, the assistant directeur sportif of Kelme, is more confident about his rider. "He'll win the sprint easily if they don't get caught, which they probably will," he says.

The weather continues to be overcast and chilly, and the crowds remain large from the start in the town of La Chatre in the center of the country south to Brive la Gaillarde.

Vasseur has instigated the attack, accelerating away from the pack at about kilometer 95 and being joined immediately by the two others. As they pass through the town of St. Junien la Brégare, 10 kilometers from the feed zone where the riders snatch bags of food on the fly, the three are working hard and the pack is riding at a leisurely pace.

This begins to pick up 40 kilometers from the finish as the sprinters' teams, led by Mario Cipollini's Saeco riders, go to the front and force the pace. TVM is also there, favoring its sprinter, Jeroen Blijlevens, as are Riso Scotti for Nicola Minali and Mapei for Jan Svorada.

The breakaway's lead begins to come down rapidly under the pressure of fresh riders rotating at the front of the pack. With 25 kilometers to go, the three are still riding hard, but only 2 minutes 5 seconds ahead.

Beucherie makes a critical decision. Another of his riders, Stuart O'Grady, is in the overall leader's yellow jersey, 1:29 ahead of Sciandri, the man Beucherie fears. He talks on his cellular phone to the Gan directeur sportif, Roger Legeay, who is trailing the main pack in another car, and they decide that they cannot risk a victory by Sciandri by perhaps a minute and a half. That and the bonus 20 seconds he would get would give him O'Grady's jersey.

With 20 kilometers to go, Beucherie pulls alongside Vasseur and tells him to stop working with the others.

"That doomed the breakaway," Vasseur says after the finish. "I hated to do it because Sciandri and Rodriguez had worked so hard, but I had my orders." He sounds resigned. A year ago, he won the yellow jersey himself on a similar stage. "I thought I might get it again today," he adds.

Australia's Stuart O'Grady is congratulated for his yellow-jersey stint by his former teammate Gilbert Duclos-Lassalle.

Sciandri is not resigned but angry. "I don't understand Gan's strategy," he says. "We could have stayed away with Vasseur's help. Without it, no chance."

Before the start he knew that this stage would be right for him: When the Oakley sunglass distributor visits the team, Sciandri tells him, "Give me a nice pair. I'll be on the front all day." Although there will be little sun, there are occasional drizzles and glare.

With 15 kilometers to go, the three are caught. Vasseur, still thinking yellow jersey, attacks almost immediately. When the pack reaches and swallows him, he slams his fist down in the air in frustration.

Led still by the sprinters' teams, the riders storm into town in a bunch. For the second successive day, Cipollini pulls away from the field and crosses the line first by half the length of a bicycle. His time is 5 hours 5 minutes 32 seconds, a speed of 40 kilometers an hour. Minali is second and Svoroda is third.

The three former companions in the breakaway are far back. Vasseur is 137th and Rodriguez 148th, both in the same time as the winner since they are among the majority of the pack that finished without a split in its ranks. At the back, there are some splits and Sciandri gets his real time behind Cipollini, 1:20.

O'Grady keeps his yellow jersey, nine seconds ahead of George Hincapie, after the Gan rider finishes third in a bonus sprint and has two seconds deducted from his overall time.

The Australian is ecstatic. "I've had a magical moment in my life," he said before the start. "I would have been thrilled to have the jersey one day and it's already been two." Now it's three.

31. The Festina Case: Part Four

THE TOUR de France expelled all nine members of Festina, after the sixth stage, when its coach finally admitted that he had conducted a "concerted" practice of supplying illegal, performance-enhancing drugs to his riders. The action was unprecedented in the world's greatest bicycle race.

Individual riders had been ousted before for offenses ranging from getting illegal tows up hills from team cars to violent actions in sprint finishes. There had also been expulsions when riders failed one of the daily drug tests—as happened to the Uzbek sprinter Djamolidine Abdoujaparov in 1997—or were caught cheating in them, but no entire team had been penalized previously on a doping charge.

At a late-night emergency news conference, Jean-Marie Leblanc cited a bylaw that said expulsion was the penalty for any action "counter to the general well-being of the race."

News of the unfolding scandal had dominated the front pages of French newspapers for the previous three days.

Leblanc spoke after conferring for nearly two hours with other officials, including Martin Bruin, the head of the race judges appointed by the UCI.

"Conditions since the race started in Dublin a week ago have been sufficiently grave for this discussion and this decision," Leblanc said. He also cited "the morality of the Tour" and "the shadow that has been cast over the race" as the scandal widened from a Festina team worker to the coach and the doctor. After he read his statement, Leblanc refused to answer questions, including those about a presumption of innocence and penalties based on an informal accusation.

Bruno Roussel, the coach, and Eric Ryckaert, the doctor, were placed under formal investigation by a French judge earlier in the day on charges of buying and transporting illegal drugs and supplying them to riders. Formal investigation is a step short of arrest but kept them in custody. They had been held and questioned by police for three days.

A lawyer for Roussel, Thibault de Montbrial, read a statement in the northern city if Lille that admitted the supply of drugs to the riders and said, "The object was to optimize performance under strict medical control," while assuring that the riders would not use drugs without such control.

Dr. Ryckaert was said to have furnished a similar admission to the investigating judge but it was not made public. No official accusation was leveled against any riders for the Festina team.

Philippe Joubert, an assistant public prosecutor in Lille, said that the riders would be questioned "as witnesses" once the Tour ended in Paris on August 2.

Reached at his hotel by phone in the south-central region of France where the race ended its sixth daily stage in Brive la Gaillarde, a Festina rider expressed shock at Roussel's statement but refused to comment further, indicating that he feared the phone lines had been tapped by the police.

After the expulsion was announced, one of the riders, the Australian Neil Stephens, sounded resigned over the phone as he said, "Frankly, I was ready to drop out tomorrow anyway. Our morale is shot, and you can't compete that way."

Miguel Rodriguez, the sponsor of the team, had warned that he would terminate his financial support immediately if the riders proved to have been using drugs. The Festina team had an annual budget of about $6 million. But "There is no question of pulling our team out of the Tour," he said as recently as the morning before Roussel's statement. "We have to let justice and investigators do their job."

32. Stage Seven: An American Dream

AFTER a week of flat roads and sprint finishes, Jan Ullrich began the real defense of his Tour de France championship in the seventh stage by blowing away the rest of the 172-man field in the day's long time trial and donning the yellow jersey. He was clocked in 1 hour 15 minutes 25 seconds over the rolling and sweltering 58-kilometer (36-mile) course from Meyrignac l'Eglise to Correze in south-central France. In a major surprise, two Americans finished second and third behind the 24-year-old German and now ranked in the top five overall. Tyler Hamilton, 27, a native of Marblehead, Mass., riding for the U.S. Postal Service team, finished in second place, 1 minute 10 seconds behind Ullrich. Bobby Julich, 26, a native of Glenwood Springs, Colo., riding for Cofidis, was third, 8 seconds behind Hamilton.

"It's the American renaissance," Julich proclaimed afterward. "This is great for American cycling."

Laurent Jalabert, 29, riding for the ONCE team in Spain and the world time trial champion, was fourth, 1:24 behind Ullrich; and Slava Ekimov, 32, a Russian with U.S. Postal Service, was fifth, 1:40 behind.

Ullrich took the overall lead from Stuart O'Grady, who dropped to eighth place. Second overall was the Dane Bo Hamburger, 1:18 behind, the same time as Julich in third place. Jalabert was fourth, Hamilton fifth, and Ekimov sixth after a memorable day for the mailmen.

"I feel strong," said Hamilton, who had lost nearly seven minutes in the previous year's first long time trial. "I've taken a step up the last couple of months." A strong climber, he was expected to remain well-placed once the race reached the Pyrenees.

Also a strong climber, Julich lost more than eight minutes in the first time trial the year before, when he was trapped by a brief rainstorm. He was exuberant this time.

"It's a dream. This isn't Redlands Classic, this isn't Cascade, this is the Tour de France."

He was equally jubilant about Hamilton's performance, saying, "I just wish I were Tyler's agent. A second place in a Tour de France time trial, that ought to be worth a million." Not that third place was to be sneered at.

"It was very, very hot," Julich said of his ride. "I had my helmet on and had to throw it off. I finished feeling not strong but decent, which is all you can expect to feel after doing a 60-kilometer time trial.

"When I look at the standings and see Tyler Hamilton and Bobby Julich in the top five—I mean, wow!" he added. "Now that we're so close, Tyler and I, one of us has to take the yellow jersey. It's been a long time coming for an American, and it's about time."

Luckily for him, Ullrich does not understand English. Even if he did, the way he rode, he should not have worried overmuch.

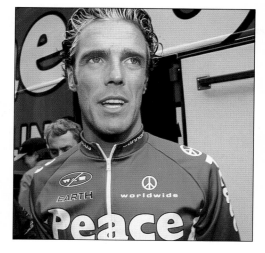

Top right: Mario Cipollini, also known as Super Mario, the Sun King, and Mario the Magnificent, displaying his special jersey to honor the Tour start in Ireland. Although he's considered the fastest man on two wheels, he was only semi-super in the 1998 Tour.

Top left: A relieved Chris Boardman smiles after winning the Prologue in the 1998 Tour. He's considered the "Prologue world champion." Once the Tour got underway, unfortunately, he soon crashed and had to abandon the race.

Below: Despite news of a drug bust within his Festina team, Swiss rider Laurent Dufaux tries to focus on the prologue.

Above: On the eve of the 1998 Tour, Festina team director Bruno Roussel tries to answer questions during an impromptu press conference in Dublin concerning the doping scandal involving his team. Although here he denies the charges, he later admitted there was systematic doping.

Below: Belgian sprinter Tom Steels proved to be the star sprinter of the 1998 Tour. The gritty racer won stages in every country the Tour visited during the race.

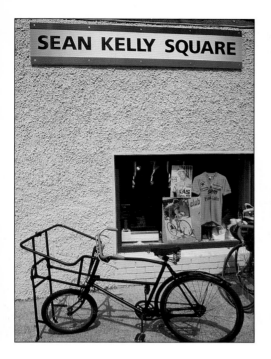

Top left: Shop windows remember their hero on Sean Kelly Square in Kelly's home town, Garrick on Suir.
Top right: Two Saeco-Cannondale riders relax before the start of the third stage in Roscoff.

Below: Veteran American rider Frankie Andreu finished his seventh Tour de France in 1998. Although he captains the U.S. Postal Service team, he is still searching for the ever-elusive stage victory.

Above: The classy German sprinter Erik Zabel, of the Deutsche Telekom Team, went on to win the green jersey for the best performance in the points classification for the third consecutive year.

Below: French boy scouts watch as the Tour passes through the Limousin region of France during the sixth stage.

Top left: Austrian rider Georg Totschnig, shown here on the Plateau de Beille climb, did his best for his Deutsche Telekom team, but couldn't help them win the yellow jersey this year.
Top right: American rider Bobby Julich stretches and meditates before the stage 7 time trial in Correze. After the 58 km time trial, he'd prove that his performance in the Prologue was no fluke.
Below: Australian rider Stuart O'Grady can hardly believe his eyes. The up-and coming 24-year-old spent three days in the yellow jersey.

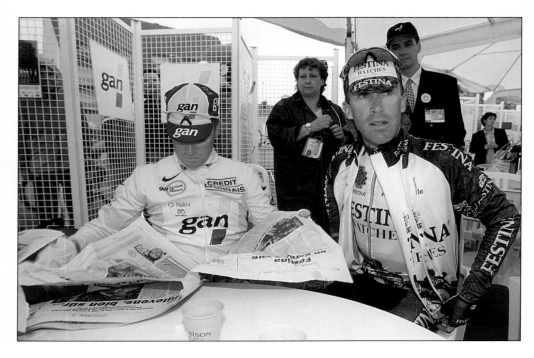

Above: Two Australians experience the 1998 Tour in very different ways. Stuart O'Grady, left, of the Gan team, savors his time in the yellow jersey, while Neil Stephens, right, of Festina, tries to ignore the stress of the drug scandal surrounding his team.

Below: The Festina team leader, Richard Virenque, gives an emotional statement to the press after his team is ejected from the Tour.

Top left: French national champion Laurent Jalabert rode strongly throughout the first week. But after finishing 4th in the stage 7 time trial, the world's number-one-ranked rider crumbled in the Alps.
Top right: After helping his Cofidis team leader Bobby Julich on the climb to Plateau de Beille on stage 11, American rider Kevin Livingstone struggles to finish. He finished 17th overall in the Tour.
Below: Jacky "The Diesel" Durand won the most aggressive rider prize in the Tour. The Casino rider was constantly on the attack, and his aggressive style gave him victory on stage 8 into Montauban.

Above: Team members celebrate the stage 9 victory with Dutchman Leon van Bon of the Rabobank team. Throughout the Tour, he was constantly on the attack, and his efforts paid off with his victory into Pau.

Below: Spanish climber Fernando Escartin attacked up the Peyresourde pass on stage 10. He was having the best Tour of his career and moved into 4th place overall after the Pyrenees and the Alps. But then his Kelme team joined the boycott of the Tour, forcing him to drop out.

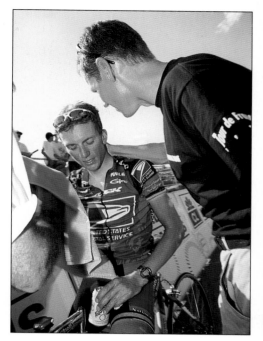

Top left: Eros "The Caboose Conductor" Poli is charged with bringing the stragglers home on time. Although he rarely wins, he is a constant crowd favorite.

Top right: After an eye-opening performance in the stage 7 time trial, Tyler Hamilton cracked on stage 9, suffering from heat exhaustion and dehydration. Coach Johnny Weltz waited to assist him.

Below: Spectators along the way encourage the riders. Here racers receive a hearty welcome from fans as they approach Carpentras on stage 13.

Above: In the Pyrenees mountains, Germany's Jan Ullrich impressed many with his powerful yet controlled riding. Insiders, however, were already predicting that the defending Tour champion was not the same vintage as the 1997 Ullrich.

Below: Marco Pantani cemented his Tour victory with this long solo ride over the legendary Galibier pass and up the summit of the Deux Alpes climb. Ullrich relinquished the yellow jersey to Pantani after he lost more than six minutes during that 15th stage.

Top left: Italy's Rodolfo Masi was having the Tour of his life. He won the grueling stage 10 in the Pyrenees. But when suspicious drugs were found in his suitcase, his Tour came to an early end.
Top right: Pantani in his best form, blasting uphill in the Pyrenees during the 11th stage.
Below: Holland's Michel Boogerd, left, of the Rabobank team, and France's Jean-Cyril Robin, right, of the U.S. Postal Service team, shown here battling up the rain-covered Galibier climb, were just two of the fresh faces in the 1998 Tour. They eventually finished 5th and 6th overall.

Above: Italy's Rodolfo Masi, left, leads France's Christophore Rinero at the foot of the Galibier climb on stage 15. For much of the Tour, Masi led the best climber competition, but the little-known Rinero was never far behind, and when Masi was forced out of the race, Rinero took over his polka-dot jersey as the King of the Mountains.

Below: Despite the support for the riders, many fans were out in protest, refusing to see their sport infested with drugs.

Top left: Up-and-coming Danish rider Bo Hamburger had his best Tour yet. He wore the yellow jersey for a day and finished 15th overall.

Top right: The weather was just one aspect of the 1998 Tour ambiance that could have been better.

Below: So suffocating had been the pressure of the yellow jersey, that Jan Ullrich appeared almost relieved when he finally lost it at the finish of the 15th stage. From the minute he stepped out of his team van each morning, he was surrounded by a crowd of journalists and photographers.

Above: Three-time Tour winner Greg LeMond came to the 1998 race as a tourist, but he was still the center of attention.

Below: On the Champs Elysées at the end of the tour, Stéphane Heulot, of La Française des Jeux, and Viatcheslav Ekimov, of U.S. Postal Service, tried to grab the stage win that had eluded them throughout the days before, and again eluded them as Tom Steels completed his collection of stage victories for a total of four in this Tour alone.

Top left: Coming down the Col de Madeleine during the 16th stage. Ullrich leads Pantani, who had just the day before captured the yellow jersey from him.

Top right: As Bobby Julich moved up in the overall standings, he had to adapt to increasing pressure from the press. Here he is shown joking with the press before the start of the 11th stage in Luchon.

Below: Smile, Marco: the Tour is over and you're the Champion. Pantani remains concentrated even as he rolls down the Champs Elysées before his victory lap.

Top left: Belgium's Axel Merckx of the Italian Polti team showed promise in his first Tour. His 10th place in the overall standings proved that the great Eddy's son can handle the job at hand.

Top right: Laurent Jalabert was sober during much of the final week's racing after his disappointing performance in the Alps, and he eventually dropped out of the Tour in the midst of the riders' strike during stage 17.

Bottom: Lance Armstrong was back in form by the time of the World Championships in October 1998.

33. Stuart O'Grady's Big Kahuna

NOT MANY riders could imagine worse conditions for their tenure in the yellow jersey than Stuart O'Grady. Rains soaked his golden fleece throughout the first day. The arrest of the team director and doctor took front page, the following day. And on his final day, the expulsion of the Festina team, one of the top teams in the 1998 Tour, again dominated.

Little matter for Stuart O'Grady, the Australian with the French Gan team. The days he spent in the yellow jersey represented nothing more and nothing less than "The Big Kahuna."

Stuart O'Grady tries to enjoy his last day in the yellow jersey, despite the grueling time trial.

"Ah heck," says the quiet but always amiable 24-year-old rider. "I know that much of the headlines these last couple of days have not been about my yellow jersey but about the Festina affair. Really though, that didn't bother me too much. It doesn't matter to me if I'm on the front page, the middle page or the real-estate page. I came here to do a job and achieve a personal dream of mine. And I did that."

As O'Grady talks, he sits in his Gan team car in a dust bowl called a parking lot. It is the finish of the Correze time trial. He has just lost the yellow jersey to Germany's Jan Ullrich. But his smile couldn't be brighter as he appeased the last of the day's many autograph seekers.

Some do not even know the name of the rider they are soliciting. Everybody, however, recognizes the yellow jersey. And O'Grady is not minding the attention. Especially since he knows it is coming to an end. "This has all been great. Just great," he says. "Who would have thought a freckly guy like me would ever be wearing a beautiful shirt like this?"

Well, for one, Roger Legeay, his team director. The legendary French director has harvested Anglophone riders on his many teams for nearly two decades. It is he who first worked with talents like Ireland's Stephen Roche and Australia's Phil Anderson.

When Legeay talks of O'Grady, he sounds as if he were describing fine silk between his fingers. "I signed Stuart very young," recalls Legeay. "He traveled 20,000 kilometers when he was only 20 years old. That really impressed me. And I've got to say that somewhere I feel like his papa. I helped him find a house, insure his car, those kinds of things.

"But I always knew it was worth it," insists Legeay. "He just had so much talent. Before he was 20 he was a world champion in the team pursuit. So from the very beginning I sketched out a career plan with him.

"With talent like that, you don't just stick him in any race where the team might need him. No, you've got to think about what is best for the rider first. I knew that one day he was going to produce a real exploit. I didn't know when that exploit would happen, but I always knew it would."

For a French directeur sportif like Legeay, on a French team like Gan, the so-called exploit could not have come at a better time than during the Tour de France. But then Legeay specializes in Tour de France results. His teams may not win the race very often, but no other team so consistently dominates the opening week as Legeay's squad.

His formula goes something like this: Place a maximum number of riders highly in the prologue, then cover all the early breakaways and contest all of the bonus sprints in an effort to capture the yellow jersey.

With the help of prologue specialists like Chris Boardman and pursuit riders like O'Grady, Legeay's formula worked like a charm in 1998.

Like in 1994 and 1997, Boardman won the prologue and the yellow jersey. And when he lost it in a crash on the second stage, O'Grady soon picked up the slack. After making the winning break on the third stage, he moved to within 3 seconds of the lead, and the next day he had little trouble picking up those precious seconds in bonus sprints to grab the jersey.

In fact, the toughest competition came not from a non-sprinter like Hamburger, but from American national champion George Hincapie, who himself was only 2 seconds from the lead at the start.

Today it has all come to an end. Yet, as team personnel try to hurry him out of the sandlot and to the hotel for his evening's massage, O'Grady is in no hurry. "It's all been great," he says with a smile still pinned to his face. "I've dreamed of this since I was a kid, since I first saw my countryman Phil Anderson with it. Now it's all over.

"Honestly though, the last three days have simply been a dream come true. It has definitely given me new objectives in my life. It has given me new perspectives on what I can expect as a professional and of myself.

"Now I need a few days of recovery. Since the prologue, I've been going 100 percent, and if I'm going to make it to Paris, I'm going to have to pull it back a notch. But if I finish last every day from now on, I'm never going to forget this Tour de France." O'Grady didn't finish last in every stage. He even went on to win the 14th stage into Grenoble. And when the Tour finally returned to Paris, his freckled face was still radiant.

34. The Festina Case: Part Five

THE TOUR de France and the expelled Festina team bid adieu in a steamy café as the race's organizers refused to yield to a demand by the riders that they be reinstated.

"If they insist on racing, their times won't be taken and it will be a charade," said Jean-Marie Leblanc after he met with six of the team's nine riders in the back room of the café Chez Gillou, in the town of Correze near the finish of the seventh stage. "They are out of the race, period," he flung over his shoulder as he hurried away.

A quarter hour after he left the café, the riders began to emerge in their blue team uniforms. Their spokesman was the team leader, Richard Virenque, an idol in his home country.

"We've been ordered out, OK, let the Tour continue without us," he said. "It has to continue because it's such a great, popular event. We asked to continue because there are no charges, no witnesses against us. They said no. This is very difficult personally and professionally for the riders. We'll continue as a team, and we'll ride the Vuelta in September," he added, referring to the three-week Vuelta à España, the Tour of Spain.

"We'll be at the start of the Tour de France next year, and we'll come to win. Vive le Tour de France 1998," Virenque concluded as his voice cracked and he began weeping.

Other riders supported the Festina team after the news was made public. "If they've been expelled to save the prestige of the Tour, it's ridiculous," said Stéphane Barthe, a Frenchman with the Casino team and a former French national champion.

"Guilt by association and innuendo isn't the way to go," said Bobby Julich after he finished third in the day's stage, a long individual time trial. "These guys haven't been proven guilty. It's bad for them and worse for the sport."

"It's very severe, and I feel sorry for the riders," said Andrea Tafi, an Italian with the Mapei team. "They're trying to make their living, nothing has been proven against them, and now they're out of the race."

He was echoed by Marino Lejaretta, a former first-class racer who now worked as an official of the ONCE team. "Our riders feel terrible about the image this is giving the sport," he said. "We're mostly Spaniards and Festina is mostly French, but we're all riders."

"It's really hard to point fingers at the riders when they're not found positive," said Marty Jemison. "You can make assumptions where these products were going, but these riders did not fail drug tests. The whole affair is terrible for the Tour and for all of us who love bicycle racing."

Italian riders other than Tafi, the national champion, were also rocked. "The Mapei team is stunned," said Freddy Viaene, a Belgian masseur with the team, which shared a hotel with Festina the night of the expulsion. "It's like a hammer is coming down on everybody, and the riders say, 'Who's next to be accused?'"

That was a good question. Although the use of illegal drugs had long been suspected in the professional pack, the thousands of drug checks carried out every season convict fewer than a dozen riders annually. A major question had been whether the rumors were unfounded or whether some of the doctors that most teams employ were far ahead of the drug inspectors.

As a Festina official, who refused to be identified, said: "We're the scapegoats. They're using us as an example for a practice that is widespread in the sport."

The public was standing by the team. After Virenque's statement, he was cheered by passersby. Handmade signs to encourage Festina dotted the long time trial course despite the absence of Festina riders. Similar signs had been seen all along the route since the drug scandal began unfolding.

There seemed to be a chance that the remaining 172 riders would conduct some sort of sympathy demonstration, as they did in 1988 when Tour leader Pedro Delgado was found guilty of using a generally banned drug to mask the use of steroids. The riders then delayed the start of a daily stage in protest until it was made clear that Delgado would be allowed to continue since his drug was not scheduled to become illegal in the sport for a few more weeks.

Riders agreed with Virenque when he said that the Tour had been under pressure to safeguard its image, but some thought a benefit might result from the exclusion.

"The scandal's a shame, it's terrible for the sport of cycling," said Tyler Hamilton, after he posted the then-best time in the individual time trial. "But maybe this is going to open some eyes and change things.

"We had to wake up at 6 o'clock this morning" when officials of the International Cycling Union conducted surprise checks of riders' levels of red blood corpuscles. A finding above 50 percent is considered proof of the use of the artificial hormone EPO.

Riders above that level are suspended for two weeks, as seven had been already in the season. The checks were carried out on 53 riders on 6 Tour teams and nobody failed them. They were the first administered since the start of the race a week before.

35. Stage Eight:
Glory for a Lesser God

JAN ULLRICH lost the yellow jersey a day after he gained it, but neither the German nor his Telekom team cared. Rather than showing any weakness, he was the victim of a tactical miscalculation.

A long, multirider breakaway was allowed to gain too much time on a blazingly hot eighth stage as the Tour moved toward the Pyrenees. As a result, the overall leader was now Laurent Desbiens, a Frenchman with Cofidis, not hitherto celebrated in song and story. He would certainly return to anonymity when the mountains began.

Second overall was Andrea Tafi, another nonclimber. Third was Jacky Durand, a Frenchman with Casino, who had even less uphill speed than Desbiens and Tafi. But give Durand a relatively flat road with no more than a handful of minor climbs, as he had on the 190.5-kilometer (118-mile) journey from Brive la Gaillarde to Montauban in the southwest, and he can motor.

Durand was timed in 4 hours 40 minutes 55 seconds, a speed of 40 kilometers an hour, as he won a sprint among the seven survivors of what had been a mass breakaway for nearly 120 kilometers. All the fugitives were far down in the standings after the long individual time trial of the previous day, and riders of that rank are often allowed to try their luck.

The principle is that such an attack neutralizes the overall leader's real rivals back in the pack while none of the men in the breakaway will gain enough time to take the yellow jersey. Back to the drawing board.

Second in the finish was Tafi, with Fabio Sacchi, an Italian with Polti, third. Desbiens, the highest ranking among the six after the time trial, did not contest the sprint, knowing that he was now the overall leader anyway. He finished fifth.

Seven minutes 45 seconds later, Ullrich and the main pack arrived. Since Desbiens had started the day 4:30 behind and gained some bonus seconds en route, he now led Tafi by 14 seconds, Durand by 43 and Joona

Looka, a Finn with Lotto and another member of the breakaway, by 2:54. In fifth place, but first in the real world, was Ullrich, 3:21 behind.

The two Americans who were previously in the top five dropped but stayed in the top 10. Bobby Julich was in seventh place and Tyler Hamilton was ninth. Both, like Ullrich, and unlike Desbiens and his comrades, can also climb.

The stage passed with no reaction to the Festina team's expulsion other than about a dozen supportive signs among the tens of thousands of fans along the route.

36. Stage Nine: Getting Ready for the Mountains

THAT wasn't Bobby Julich whom the Cofidis team sent ahead to protect its interests when a handful of low-ranked riders went on a long breakaway for the second successive day in the Tour. Joining breakaways like that is the work of a domestique, a servant in French, and Julich was now anything but.

After his 17th-place finish in the last Tour, his fourth place in the prologue in Dublin, and his third place in the first long individual time trial, this was the new, improved Bobby Julich model in the world's greatest bicycle race. His domestique days were over and he now ranked as a co-leader of his Cofidis team.

He was careful to be politic in defining his role: "I expect to be strong enough to support Francesco Casagrande," the nominal team leader, "in the mountains—and to finish better than I did last year."

But now that he was in seventh place overall just before the mountains, where he was expected to shine, his goals were really bigger. "This is only my second Tour, and I'm still learning," he said before the start of the ninth stage, 210 steamy kilometers (130 steamy miles) from charming Montauban to hospitable Pau, the doorstep to the Pyrenees.

"Learning is all that matters," he continued. "I may not win the Tour de France this year, but I hope to win it in the future. You put these experiences in the bank and learn from them."

Julich protected his high ranking by crossing the line in 31st place in the same time as all the other major contenders. Less fortunate was the other American rider who had been in the top 10: Tyler Hamilton suffered a heatstroke as the temperature reached 40 degrees Celsius (104 degrees Fahrenheit) and lost 18 minutes 18 seconds.

"We thought he was gone, would have to drop out," said teammate Marty Jemison. Hamilton fell to 160th place among the 168 riders remaining of the 189 who started the Tour.

The winner after a 170-kilometer breakaway was Leon van Bon, a Dutchman with Rabobank, who beat Jens Voigt, a German with Gan, by half a wheel in the time of 5 hours 21 minutes 10 seconds, a speed of 39 kilometers an hour.

Third was Massimiliano Lelli, the Cofidis domestique who sped across to the breakaway and stayed with it in case it gained so much time that it took the yellow jersey away from Laurent Desbiens. In that case, the team would have another rider at or near the top.

Despite heroic efforts of Voigt, however, the main pack finished just 12 seconds behind. The breakaway's lead topped out at 4 minutes and change, which was no threat to Desbiens, since all the men in front were many more minutes behind him at the start.

Voigt, who began the original acceleration, did most of the work over the rolling course, frequently dousing his head with water bottles passed to him by fans. He originated the final sprint about 200 meters from the line and could not quite hold off van Bon, who passed the finish with his arms uplifted while the German was slumped, shouting in frustration.

Desbiens retained the yellow jersey by 14 seconds over Andrea Tafi, who twice tried to speed away and gain that precious time. He failed. Third overall was Jacky Durand, 43 seconds behind. They all were doomed to disappear early in the Pyrenees.

Julich knew before the stage that if a multirider breakaway occurred, he was not expected to chase it. "That's not my job today," he said. "My job is tomorrow." The riders, minus the Italian sprinter Mario Cipollini, who dropped out during the stage—as always, before the mountains, despite his pre-Tour talk of the green points jersey and the finish in Paris—faced four big climbs the next day and four more the day after.

"I'm looking forward to the mountains," Julich said, noting that he lost 22 minutes in the previous Tour in the first day of climbing in the Pyrenees. "Last year I was scared of them," he admitted. He came back strong in the final week, especially in the first stage in the Alps and the last long time trial.

"The memories that I have of the last week in the last Tour are fantastic, and those are mainly in the mountains. That's what I want to feel again. Last year it was a question of morale," he explained. "I was very nervous last year in the first two weeks, but this year from the start I've felt very relaxed and very motivated.

"The time trial did a lot for my confidence. The prologue did a lot for my confidence. Phase One is complete: I had a good prologue, stayed out of trouble in the crashes and had a good time trial. I'm happy. Mission accomplished. The Pyrenees aren't quite my style—I like more the Alps. But I'm ready."

"You've got to be strong right away," Julich said. "This year I've pushed myself a little bit more on the smaller climbs, tested myself in the time trial, and worked harder in some of the bonus sprints. The object was to get ready for the mountains. This year I'm ready for them, I think. I hope."

37. Stage 10:
The Natural Order of Things

JAN ULLRICH, Bobby Julich, Bo Hamburger, Laurent Jalabert, and Luc Leblanc in the first five places overall—the Tour de France entered the Pyrenees mountains and a sense of order returned to the standings.

Gone were Laurent Desbiens, Andrea Tafi, and Jacky Durand, who ruled the roost during the previous few days and now were no higher than Tafi's 54th place. Proving that anything is possible with enough courage and savvy, however, an unlikely winner emerged after the 196.5-kilometer (122-mile) stage across the fabled "Circle of Death" peaks.

That was Rodolfo Massi, an Italian with Casino and not one of the major climbers. He benefited from a long breakaway with Cédric Vasseur and Alberto Elli, another Italian with Casino, to give the French team its second victory in 10 stages.

Massi did no work during most of the breakaway from the first climb, the daunting Aubisque peak, rated beyond category in difficulty, through the second climb, the similarly rated Tourmalet. Team strategy called for him to ride in the slipstream of Elli and Vasseur, saving his strength for the last two climbs, the Aspin and the Peyresourde, both rated first category, or a notch lower than their predecessors.

On the fourth climb, Massi took off, leaving his weary teammate and the unwitting Vasseur behind. Massi had enough power left to hold off a late charge by the Italian Marco Pantani of Mercatone Uno, the winner of the Giro d'Italia and—on any of the 364 other days of the year—a far superior climber to Massi.

But Pantani, who fell on the frigid descent from the Aubisque, then reverted to his habit of unleashing his charge too late, and once again finished a Tour stage in second place. The winner was timed in 5 hours 49 minutes 40 seconds, a speed of 33 kilometers an hour, or 36 seconds faster than Pantani across the finish line after a 15-kilometer descent from the Peyresourde into Luchon.

Third in the stage, which started in Pau, was Michael Boogerd, a Dutchman with Rabobank, 59 seconds behind. Clocking the same time were nine other riders, including Ullrich, Julich, and Leblanc—not the one who was Tour director but a French rider with Polti.

Ullrich regained the overall leader's yellow jersey that he yielded to Desbiens three days earlier. Overall, the German was 1:18 ahead of Julich. Hamburger was third, 2:17 behind the leader, with Jalabert 2:38 behind and Leblanc 3:03 behind. The 151 remaining riders got another chance to climb the next day before the Tour took its only day off.

An ecstatic Julich attempted to be blasé afterward. "Last year I had goosebumps when I finished with the leaders in Morzine," he said. "This time I knew my place was with the best."

Seventeen riders quit the race in the Pyrenees, some out of exhaustion, some because of crashes on foggy and slippery roads. The major casualty was Francesco Casagrande, the Italian leader of Cofidis, whom Julich had been obligated to work for. With Casagrande gone, the American became the team leader for whom everybody else works.

"Everybody" included another American with Cofidis, Kevin Livingston, a strong climber who finished 14th in the stage, 1:58 behind, and ranked 18th overall, 5:38 behind. He was likely to excel the next day in the final climb to the Plateau de Beille, which was making its debut in the Tour but which Livingston knew from his second-place finish in 1997 in the Tour de l'Avenir.

The weather turned overnight, dropping from a reading of 40 degrees Celsius (104 degrees Fahrenheit) to half that atop the climbs. A heavy fog and swirling mist, especially on the first climb, contributed to the difficulties, making descents from the four peaks treacherous.

Another key factor in the stage was the absence of the expelled Festina team. The team's nine riders are usually dominant in the mountains and would surely have attacked Ullrich and the other favorites early in the stage.

"I think it will be difficult to find a challenger, to have the numbers in the front to test the Telekom guys," said a prescient Frankie Andreu beforehand. "Festina could put five or six riders up there and get Telekom in trouble. Now I think it's going to be more of an open race."

Not even Andreu could have foreseen a victory by Massi, but otherwise his prediction was spot on.

Tyler Hamilton, who had lost more than 18 minutes the day before when he suffered a heatstroke and crossed the finish line in a daze, started and finished the 10th stage.

"I was suffering so bad," Hamilton said in a drizzle at the start in Pau. "I wasn't delirious, but I was pretty out of it. It was extremely hot and I was completely empty. My body just shut down."

He explained that he had suffered stomach troubles for the last month and that some days he could not retain food or drink. The ninth stage was one of those days. "I went from such a high to such a low in two days," he continued, referring to his second place in the individual time trial to his 160th place two days later.

Nevertheless, he was game to see how he would do in the Pyrenees. "I put my body through a lot yesterday," he said. "How it reacts today I don't know. You can only push your body so hard and then it doesn't want to go any harder."

Hamilton finished the mountain stage in 126th place among a big group of riders bringing up the rear, 31:34 behind Massi. In his way, he rode just as courageous a race as the winner.

38. Stage 11: Pantani Comes Out

MARCO Pantani had been saying for months that this was not a Tour de France for climbers, among whom he was far and away the best. Not demanding enough, he insisted, not enough mountains, not enough finishes on peaks to deprive lesser climbers of their chance to make up lost time on long descents.

Enough enoughs, or basta, as the Italian leader of the Mercatone Uno team would say. Pantani rode a wonderful race in the 11th stage, timing his acceleration away from the pack exactly right, and climbing with nimble ease to win the last of two stages in the Pyrenees.

He finished 1 minute 26 seconds ahead after the 170-kilometer (105-mile) slog from Luchon to the dusty and uninhabited Plateau de Beille, as the sun returned and the temperature rose to the high 80s Fahrenheit.

Pantani also rose—from 11th to fourth place overall with the Alps, his other playground, still to come. Three days of climbing there would start in a few days..

How about Bobby Julich, though? The American came in third and solidified his hold on second place overall by finishing 7 seconds ahead of Jan Ullrich, the man in the yellow jersey.

"I felt comfortable during the last climb," 16 steep kilometers rated beyond category in difficulty, Julich reported. "I even felt stronger at the top," where he left Ullrich behind in the final kilometer. "I rode a cautious race," Julich continued. "I've got to lay it on the line in the Alps and see if I can't win this thing."

He now trailed Ullrich by 1:11. Third overall was Laurent Jalabert, 3:01 behind—the same deficit that Pantani had in fourth place. Another favorite, Abraham Olano, the Spanish leader of the Banesto team, quit during the stage because of injuries in a crash the day before. And what about Ullrich? He labored mightily at the front of the pack chasing Pantani up the final ascent, setting a strong pace with Julich on his back wheel. At one point, the German had a flat, changed his wheel, looked around for a teammate, found nobody, and carried on the pursuit himself, perhaps unwisely. Later, he was scolded royally by his directeur sportif, Walter Godefroot, for a mistake of youth in not waiting for help.

Even when he faltered, he still finished eighth in the 149-man field. After all his troubles with weight and lost racing time during the spring, Ullrich had come through the Pyrenees in yellow and looked strong. Many riders, including Julich, had been warning that Pantani could become his main rival, but that might depend on the final time trial, a day before the finish in Paris, where Ullrich would be heavily favored.

A lot would also depend on how well Julich bore the pressure in only his second Tour. After the crash, injury, and withdrawal of Francesco Casagrande, Julich headed the Casino team. His troops included two other riders who excelled in the 11th stage: Roland Meier, a Swiss, finished second after a long breakaway and Kevin Livingston finished ninth, 2:01 behind Pantani.

Cofidis, a team in its second year and one with few results earlier during the season, now had Julich in second place, Meier in ninth, Livingston in 11th, and Christophe Rinero in 12th—and all were strong climbers.

Nobody climbs faster than Pantani, however. He proved that once again with his fifth Tour de France stage victory and his triumph a month before in the three-week Giro d'Italia, where he crushed the pack in the mountains.

"He's got great class, Pantani, a truly great climber," said another of that breed, Lucien Van Impe, who won the Tour in 1976. Now a driver for a Belgian newspaper's car in the race, van Impe bubbled over with praise for the Italian. "He's alone, the best in the world right now."

But Pantani does tend sometimes to accelerate too late, as he did the day before, when he finished second after a long descent in which he could not overtake the leader.

"That's because he doesn't always use his head," Van Impe said. "That's his problem: He climbs with his legs, not always with his head."

Not a problem this day: Pantani sped away from about 20 riders after a kilometer or two of the final climb and just kept speeding away. He overtook Meier, who had led him by 4 minutes earlier, within 5 kilometers and rushed to the summit, pausing only to pour fans' bottles of water over his shaven head.

With the heavy fog of the previous day gone, the stage across the Pyrenees afforded gorgeous views of the forested mountains and their villages of gray stone houses and slate roofs. The sky was a flawless baby blue and the pastoral quality of the day rang with the sound of bells from grazing herds of cattle.

There was a solemn sense to the stage as well. The pack paused at kilometer 40 while flowers were laid at the monument to Fabio Casartelli, the Italian rider with Motorola who died after a crash there on July 18, 1995, a month short of his 25th birthday.

Shortly thereafter, Meier attacked. Large crowds applauded him en route and passengers on a train that briefly ran alongside the course leaned out the windows to cheer him on. The Swiss had a good thing going for him—until Pantani used his head.

39. The Festina Case: Part Six

THE DRUG scandal enveloping the sport and the Tour widened as three more officials and nine riders of the Festina team were taken into judicial custody and four officials of a Dutch team were questioned by the police.

The three Festina officials were two assistant coaches, Miguel Moreno and Michel Gros, and the team's manager, Joel Chabiron. Also held were the nine riders who started the Tour. They all were ordered detained in Lyon pending a judge's decision whether to place them under formal investigation. They were not placed under formal arrest but spent the night in a police station's cells, naked and alone.

The riders, expelled from the Tour after their coach said from jail that he had supplied them with illegal performance-enhancing drugs, denied any guilt. The team's jailed doctor had since said that the riders contributed a total of $70,000 to a pool to buy the drugs, which they again denied. "The riders were obliged to put part of their victory bonuses into a 'black box' fund to buy banned substances," said the doctor, Eric Ryckaert, through his lawyer. "These products, like regular drugs, were held at Festina's headquarters in Lyon."

The Festina officials and riders in custody joined the team's directeur sportif, its doctor, and veteran soigneur Willy Voet, who had been arrested earlier. In a parallel case, a car bearing the insignia of the TVM team from the Netherlands had been seized by the police in March near the French city of Reims and was said to be bearing drugs.

Although at the time, two mechanics were arrested and a quantity of the artificial hormone EPO was found, the case languished until the Tour's one day off, four months later. About 8 A.M. "the police arrived at our hotel while we were at breakfast and took away" the team's coach, Cees Priem, its doctor, Andrei Mihailov, and an unidentified mechanic, according to Guido van Calster, the team's manager and a former Tour rider.

An assistant coach, Hendrik Redant, was brought in for questioning later in the day and then released along with the mechanic. The two others were held in the police station of Pamiers, where the TVM team was staying in Hotel de la Rocade

TVM started the year in eighth position among the approximately 40 professional racing teams. Its annual budget, supplied by an insurance company, was a bit below $4 million, or $2 million less than Festina's.

Tour officials said the day before that they had no plans to expel the seven TVM riders remaining of the nine that had started the race. The reason, the officials said, was that no formal charges had been brought against anybody on the team and that no official had said the team was involved with drugs, unlike the Festina case.

Confirming a report in the newspaper *Le Parisien*, a judge in Ghent, Belgium, Eric Van de Sijpe, said that he could confirm that the Festina riders had used EPO. Judge Van de Sijpe conducted an inquiry in March into a pharmacist who was found to have sold large quantities of EPO, and among his alleged buyers was Dr. Ryckaert of Festina. His computer records were copied by the judge.

"I seized the riders' medical files, and in them there are indications that they used EPO," news agencies quoted the judge having said. "It's there in writing."

Some Festina officials and riders had charged that they had been made scapegoats for a practice that was widespread in the pack.

Qualified confirmation was made by Dr. Max Testa, the Asics team doctor and former doctor of the 7-Eleven team and its successor, Motorola. In an interview, he said, "I'm not really in a good position to say, since I was working 11 years with American teams and they're clean." The Motorola team left the sport in 1996.

"In Europe, drug use is quite prevalent. I would say at least 20 to 30 percent of professional riders do it. Part of the reason is the pressure of all the races, the difficulty of finding a job. You always have to be good. EPO, even if it is not detectable, is a strong risk for riders because there is a lot of data about how dangerous it is. The general situation is probably that it is mainly used by the weakest riders. They're the ones who feel they need an edge."

40. Stage 12: The Tour in Doubt

THE TOUR de France nearly unraveled as five expelled riders admitted they had used illegal drugs, a second team was warned about possible ouster, and the 150 remaining riders went on strike for two hours to protest what they considered to be harassment in the doping scandal surrounding the race.

"If the stage had been canceled, it might have been the end of the 1998 Tour," said Jean-Marie Leblanc, the race director.

"The riders showed they're fed up" with media hounding and criticism, he added in a news conference after the 12th stage was held. Leblanc especially cited a French television segment that examined the garbage of the Asics team from Italy and displayed medical paraphernalia, including syringes.

Hours before the riders refused to start, three members of the expelled Festina team, including the world road race champion, Laurent Brochard, and a two-time winner of the Vuelta, Alex Zulle, admitted to the police that they had used drugs. Two other members of the nine-man team had confessed the night before.

"I feel a great sense of relief at having confessed," said one rider, Armin Meier, a Swiss. "But I feel victimized. It's like everybody is driving 100 kilometers an hour on a highway with a 90-kilometer limit and they pull only us over."

Meanwhile, the police continued to hold two officials of the TVM team, and a magistrate said that a search of that team's hotel had revealed "a large quantity" of "doping products" and masking agents.

Leblanc warned in a statement before his news conference that he and the International Cycling Union were "extremely attentive to developments in the TVM investigation."

"If it is revealed that this team has not respected the rules and the ethics of the Tour de France and the International Cycling Union, the team will be immediately expelled," he said.

In a climate of innuendo, rumor, and anger, widespread doping practices long suspected in the sport were surfacing in its showpiece. The Tour was not only the richest and most prestigious race but also an integral part of French culture, watched by hundreds of thousands of fans at the side of the road every day and by millions on television.

Leblanc used the popularity of the race when he talked the riders into starting, he said. "We negotiated with the riders, we explained our position. We cited the multitude of fans who were awaiting them to encourage the riders and show their appreciation. In the end, they understood."

Whether the riders would demonstrate the next morning was uncertain. Leblanc said he would attend a meeting beforehand with an official of the International Cycling Union and representatives of the 20 teams in the race.

Three Spanish teams—Banesto, ONCE, and Vitalicio—and the Mercatone Uno team from Italy were reported to have led the strike.

"There's been some pretty harsh stuff in the Spanish media, and a lot of the riders were hurt by it," said Stuart O'Grady. "It cut deep. A lot of teams didn't want to take part in the race today."

In the central French city of Lyon, meanwhile, the nine members of the Festina team plus three of its officials who had been in custody were released. Apart from the five riders who confessed, Richard Virenque, the team leader and the second-place finisher in the previous Tour, was continuing to deny that he had been involved in a systematic program of doping.

Citing media attention to the case and the Festina riders' objections that they had been treated harshly by the police, the riders who gathered for the start of the 12th stage, in the town of Tarascon sur Ariège in the Pyrenees, decided they had had enough.

They slowly rolled 3.2 kilometers (2 miles) from the ceremonial start to the real one and then stopped, dismounting from their bicycles.

Laurent Jalabert approached Leblanc in his lead car and spoke with him. "Since the start of this Tour we have talked only about scandal and not sport," he said. "The riders are disgusted. We have been treated like cattle, and we will act like cattle and not race today. Nobody is interested in the sport side of the race. We won't ride. It's finished."

Standing and sprawled on the road, the riders conferred among themselves and with their coaches. "I'm so sick and tired of everybody being blamed for what Festina did," said Frankie Andreu. He favored not racing.

Erik Zabel, the wearer of the points leader's green jersey, said: "When Ben Johnson was caught in the '88 Olympics, only Johnson was thrown out. People didn't think all the other runners were guilty, the way they think all the cyclists are."

After an hour, the riders were persuaded to start, but they rolled so slowly that they covered only 16 kilometers in the next hour. Then the racing started in earnest with bursts of accelerations. Jalabert went on a long attack with two other riders, including his brother Nicolas of Cofidis, because he was so angry that the pack had agreed to start that he wanted it to suffer at high speed in the sultry heat. "They want to race, we'll make them race," he said.

At the finish of the 222-kilometer journey from Tarascon sur Ariège in the mountains to the unhandsome Mediterranean resort of le Cap d'Agde, Tom Steels was the clear winner ahead of François Simon, a Frenchman with Gan, and Stéphan Barthe.

Clocked in 4 hours 12 minutes 51 seconds, Steels and most of the rest of the pack rode at an amazing speed of nearly 49 kilometers an hour. Despite the two-hour delay by the strike, the pack finished only an hour behind its fastest predicted time.

This was not the first strike by riders. In 1978, they refused to cross a finish line to protest long transfers between daily stages, and in 1991 they refused for a while to start a stage to protest the mandatory wearing of helmets. In both instances, the Tour softened its rules.

In another legal development, Patrick Kiel, the magistrate who had been leading the Festina investigation in Lille, released "under strict conditions" Willy Voet, the soigneur whose arrest unleashed the drug scandal.

In an editorial about the race, the newspaper *Le Monde* said, "The 1998 Tour is finished. It is a race without faith or law. If it dies it will bury our childhood dreams with it."

In response, the French minister for sport, Marie-George Buffet, said, "The Tour is seriously ill, but there's no reason to kill it."

Whom would the riders listen to?

41. Stage 13:
The Tour Survives Itself

A TRUCE was declared the next morning, allowing the race to continue with no threat of disruption by the riders. Officials of the Tour and the International Cycling Union met with representatives of the 20 teams, and they decided to carry on with the three-week race and to hold further talks at the end of the season in October.

They also decided to "coordinate"—a deliberately vague word—policies to counter the drug scandal that had blackened the sport and threatened the Tour itself.

Daniel Baal, first vice president of the UCI, called on the international media to focus on the sporting aspect of the race rather than the doping affair that had caused one team, Festina, to be expelled and had placed another, TVM, on alert that it might be expelled.

Two officials of the TVM team continued to be held in police custody in the Pyrenees. A search of the team's hotel had revealed "doping materials" and illegal masking agents, according to a magistrate there. The officials were Cees Priem, the team's directeur sportif, and Andrei Mihailov, the team's doctor. Judicial authorities announced that the two would be transferred to the French city of Reims, where the police had arrested two TVM mechanics in March and found a quantity of illegal performance-enhancing drugs in their team car.

Public reaction to the scandal was mixed. While there was an immense crowd at the start, fans along the route appeared to be fewer than usual, especially for a Saturday. An opinion poll in the newspaper *France-Soir* said that 57 percent of the respondents thought the Tour should continue and 39 percent thought it should be halted.

"There's no reason the Tour shouldn't continue," Baal said after the meeting. "It's a demanding job, and the riders deserve our respect."

Shortly thereafter, the 147 riders rolled out of the Mediterranean resort of Frontignan la Peyrade on a 196-kilometer (121-mile) slog upcountry in heavy heat to Carpentras in Provence.

In a sprint finish among the six survivors of a long 12-man breakaway, Daniele Nardello, an Italian with Mapei, edged Vicente Garcia-Acosta, a Spaniard with Banesto. The winner of the 13th stage was timed in 4 hours 32 minutes 46 seconds, a speed of 43 kilometers an hour on a day when anybody with sense moved slowly and stayed in the shade. Fifth across the line was Marty Jemison, who dug deep in the sprint but finished a bicycle length behind.

Jan Ullrich continued to wear the yellow jersey by crossing the line in the main pack, 2:51 behind the winner. There was no change in the top five overall standings although Frenchman Stéphane Heulot, riding for La Française des Jeux, rose from 20th place to eighth by participating in the long breakaway.

On the day's only climb, Ullrich benefited from the work of his Danish teammate Bjarne Riis, winner of the 1996 Tour, who went to the front and rallied Telekom when the German's rivals showed signs of attacking.

Riis had reverted to a road captain, the rider who dictates tactics in the heat of action when the directeur sportif is unavailable. Road captains do not win the Tour de France, Riis's only goal, but help others win it.

"I'm here to win," he had said in Dublin. "My goal is to win the race, to be in yellow in Paris."

The 34-year-old Dane was speaking at a Telekom team presentation in Dublin Castle in a hall lined with portraits of dukes, earls, and other grandees. The next speaker was Ullrich, a decade younger than Riis and the defending champion.

"My goal is to win the race, to be in yellow in Paris," Ullrich said, echoing his teammate.

Something had to give, and it was Riis. Now in 15th place, seven minutes behind Ullrich, the Dane was told by team officials on the day off that he could no longer ride for himself but had to dedicate himself to his leader.

Riis knew his new role well since it was for so long his old role. Until two years before, he was road captain of teams in France and Italy. After he finished third in the 1995 Tour, he moved as the leader to Telekom.

In 1996, he won the Tour while the unheralded Ullrich finished second. In 1997 the German was an easy winner, while the Dane finished seventh, 26 minutes behind.

"I wanted to win the Tour," Riis said when he was told that he was becoming road captain again. "But with those seven minutes separating us, I have no choice.

"I have total confidence in Jan," he added. "He's very strong now." That was spoken like a road captain, not a rival.

42. Stage 14: What Doping Scandal?

AGREEING with bicycle racing authorities to sit down and discuss the sport's pharmacological problems late in the fall and deciding not to talk now about anything but the athletic aspect of the Tour de France, the 147 remaining riders continued to roll toward their rendezvous with the Alps. If teams had psychologists instead of sports doctors, they would have said that the race was in a state of denial.

Unmentioned by anybody on two wheels was the fact that two jailed officials of the TVM team were due to be transferred to Reims for questioning about the police seizure in March of a team car carrying illegal performance-enhancing drugs. If the officials implicated the team, Tour officials said, it would be expelled.

Nevertheless the riders had closed ranks. "It's a bike race and we're here to do the bike race and that's all I'll talk about," said one rider in a typical comment. He declined to be identified.

Frankie Andreu explained the general position. "I understand the drug story is part of the Tour, but it's been more than a week: It's time the drug story stops and the Tour de France gets going."

Andreu, who had completed all six of his previous Tours and finished a noble fourth in the Olympic road race in Atlanta in 1996, said he was impressed with at least three of the overall leaders a day before the race entered the Alps for three testing stages.

Of Jan Ullrich, the overall leader, Andreu said, "I think he looks strong. He looks good, maybe not as good as last year, but he's going to be hard to beat."

Bobby Julich, who ranked second overall, also drew praise from Andreu, his teammate the year before at Cofidis and at Motorola for two years before that. "Bobby looks great," he said. "He's just waiting for the Alps to try to do something. Like Ullrich, he looks very comfortable."

Marco Pantani, the Italian leader of Mercatone Uno, fourth ranked and the acknowledged king of the mountains, drew Andreu's enthusiastic praise, although he tempered it by noting that Pantani was not a time trial rider in Ullrich's and Julich's class.

"He's incredible," Andreu said. "I don't know about the final time trial, but I think he can take some time back in the mountains to make a difference."

All three leaders retained their positions after the 14th stage as a six-man breakaway by low-ranked riders was allowed to gather steam at kilometer 56 of 186.5 (116 miles) and roll unhindered over a big climb and then into Grenoble, the doorstep to the Alps.

In a sprint finish, the winner was Stuart O'Grady, the wearer of the yellow jersey for three days a week previously. He had since sunk to 91st position, more than 58 minutes behind Ullrich.

"This does it all," he said exuberantly afterward. "I wore the jersey and wanted to get in a long break and have a chance to win a stage. For me, this Tour is Disneyland."

He was timed in 4 hours 30 minutes 53 seconds, a speed of 41 kilometers. The first six finished 10:05 ahead of the main pack and O'Grady rose to 78th place.

The weather continued to be hot and muggy, but as compensation the route passed through wonderful countryside, including fields of lavender scenting the air below the mountains of the Vercors plateau. If only Cézanne had moved his easel about 100 kilometers northeast of his favored Provence near the start of the stage in Valreas.

Anyway, second in the sprint before he was set back to sixth for interference was Giuseppe Calcaterra, an Italian with Saeco. The new second-place finisher was Orlando Rodrigues, a Portuguese with Banesto, with Dutchman Leon Van Bon third.

For the second successive day, U.S. Postal Service had a rider in the breakaway, but again the mailmen's hopes were marked, as the old Elvis song put it, "Return to Sender." Peter Meinert-Nielsen, a Dane, was impressively strong, as Marty Jemison was the day before, but he also came up a little short in the final dash to the line, finishing fifth until he was elevated to fourth due to Calcaterra's demotion.

Andreu dreams of being the Postal Service rider in the break that gets away. "I'm trying to win something or do something," he said. "In the mountains the same guys win, in the mass sprints the same guys win, so the other days are the ones you really have to concentrate on. It's difficult.

"Making that break takes a bit of luck and a bit of form," he continued. "You can join 20 attacks and sometimes it's the 21st that goes. You've got to gamble and time it right. You go, go, go, go, and sometimes it happens." Not for the next three days, however. Andreu was strong and smart but no climber.

43. Nails For Breakfast

HE EATS nails for breakfast. At least that is what his teammates and friends claim. And after Stage 14, Marty Jemison looked as though he had just munched some nails.

Empty and wasted, Jemison considered his fate. He had come a long way to finish only fifth in a stage of the Tour de France. Little matter that this was only his second Tour. Little matter that he had been in a long breakaway during one of the hottest stages. Little matter that Jemison was sprinting against more experienced riders such as Italy's Andrea Tafi or France's Stéphane Heulot. The U.S. Postal Service rider was sprinting for the biggest win of his career.

He would accept no excuses. The slow-motion replay Jemison carried out in his head only convinced him that he could have won the stage. If only he had played the sprint differently. And nail-tough guys like Jemison don't take defeat easily.

Jemison, don't forget, has been racing against the odds for nearly his entire cycling career. By conventional standards, Jemison started cycling too late. Not until the age of 22, after graduating from the University of Utah in 1986, did he get serious about the sport. Yet despite a balancing act between three jobs, he got immediate results.

Already though, he was too old to garner much attention from the U.S. Cycling Federation. Instead, he moved to France with his soon-to-be wife Jill. Without solid connections, he rode virtually alone for the little-known Chateaubriant club on the border of Brittany and Normandy in 1991 and 1992.

Jill, now a public relations official with the team, laughs when she remembers the lodging provided by the club, which was minimal at best. "I'll never forget that place. Wallpaper was peeling off the walls. I think the place was actually scheduled for demolition. Ah, but we were just so happy simply to have a place. It was a great experience. Marty always believed in racing in Europe, and the people were very supportive."

Again Jemison was going against the odds. As an independent amateur, he was constantly riding against the numerous organized combines so rampant in Brittany. The combines, often referred to as the "mafia," consisted of numerous riders on various teams who tried to control the racing, and thus the prize earnings.

For an outsider, the odds were slim. But Jemison liked the odds. And he reveled in his reputation as a guy who would go up against the mafia.

The learning experience paid off. He returned to the U.S. in 1992 and nearly qualified for the Olympic team. In 1993 he won the U.S. Amateur championships and earned a place on WordPerfect, one of the top European professional teams. Apparently, however, the Dutch team did not know how to use Jemison. "The whole year was last minute," he recalls. "I got to race some great races, but I never knew until the last minute, so I could never prepare for them properly."

Finally, as with Chateaubriant, the time spent with WordPerfect would be regarded as a learning experience.

Not until he signed up with Montgomery-Bell, the forerunner to the U.S. Postal Service team, did Jemison finally secure the spot he was looking for. Throughout most of the year he is one of the team's workhorses, one of the guys who sets up the plays for others. And in that role he is virtually inexhaustible.

"You know, in the nine years I've been with Marty, I think he has dropped out of maybe five races," says Jill. "I don't know where he gets that drive. I guess it is just in his blood. Heck, his father went 30 years without missing a day of work. Whatever, there is something about Marty that drives him. It's funny, but it seems that the easier the race is, the worse he does."

During the 1998 Tour, Jemison was 33. Yet despite the age factor, he insists that he is still young on a bike. "You know, I really believe I'm a late bloomer," Jemison says as he puts his career in perspective. "Already in my amateur days, people have been telling me that I'm too old. So it's been drilled into me that I don't have time to waste."

Then finally, when he thinks back about stage 14, he cuts himself a little slack and tries to view his defeat positively. "Sure I'm frustrated that I didn't win that Tour stage. But a ride like that opens doors, and it gives me a lot of confidence for the future. One thing is for sure. Come 1999, I'll be racing even more aggressively."

44. Stage 15: Into the Alps

CLIMBING with startling power in heavy rain, Marco Pantani exploded the Tour de France as he finished alone in the Alps after an epic performance and soared from fourth place overall into the yellow jersey by nearly four minutes.

Pantani was magnificent. He bolted away from the main group of favorites halfway up the third of four major climbs, overtook an early breakaway, and then rocketed up the final climb with nobody able to keep him in sight.

He finished the 189-kilometer (117-mile) trip from Grenoble to the resort of Les Deux Alpes in 5 hours 43 minutes 45 seconds, a speed of 32.9 kilometers an hour over mountain roads shrouded in fog and slick with

American rider Marty Jemison going it alone over the Croix de Fer pass in the Alps on stage 15.

the daylong rain. So slippery were the conditions that the lightweight Pantani skidded and fell on the first climb. Obviously he recovered.

His main victim in the remaining 141-man field was Jan Ullrich, the overall leader when the stage started. After working hard all day, Ullrich faded severely in the last climb, suffering from the cold since he had neglected to don a warm jacket for the final long descent in temperatures around 40 degrees Fahrenheit. Pantani, on the other hand, took the time to stop at the top of the descent and pull on a long plastic raincoat.

Ullrich finished 25th, 8:57 behind the winner. Since he led Pantani by 3:01 at the start of the stage, that translated into a deficit of 5:56 for the German, who was now in fourth place overall.

Bobby Julich held on to second place overall by finishing fifth, 5:43 behind. He trailed Pantani by 3:53.

Il Pirata, the Pirate, as Pantani styles himself, did not win the Tour in this stage, because he still faced two more days in the Alps and then a long individual time trial the day before the race would end in Paris. But he took a credible option on victory in the same manner in which he won the Giro d'Italia the previous month.

In that race, he demolished his rivals in the mountains and then surpassed himself to finish third in the time trial, his weak point. "I don't want to talk now about the time trial," he said after this 15th of 21 daily stages. "Let me enjoy myself first on the day of my greatest victory. I didn't come to the Tour expecting to win it," he continued, "because it really isn't suited for climbers."

The remark drew a laugh from his listeners even though he had been saying this for months, complaining that the mountain stages were not difficult enough and that only two ended on a peak, as this stage did. "But now that I've got the yellow jersey," Pantani said, "I'll try to wear it to Paris."

His chances of doing that were rated excellent by Bernard Quilfen, the Cofidis directeur sportif. "We saw what he can do in a time trial in the pink jersey" of the Giro, Quilfen said. "Who knows what he's capable of in yellow."

Julich, the best-placed rider of his team, however, was not conceding victory. "The weather really bothered me," he said, "and I didn't have a good day." He noted that he nearly crashed on the final descent when the road turned right but he swerved left as he tried to don a rain jacket to keep him warm on the fast run downhill.

Asked if he intended to shadow Pantani as he had Ullrich, Julich said: "Only if I want to finish second. If I want to win, I have to attack Pantani."

Easier said than done. This was the second mountain victory in the 85th Tour for the 28-year-old Pantani, who sports an earring, a goatee, and a bandana over his shaven head. He also won in the Pyrenees after finishing second the day before when he accelerated too late in the stage and could not quite catch an early leader, Rodolfo Massi of Casino.

His timing this day was exemplary. After staying with the main group over the first climb, the Croix de Fer's 24.5 kilometers with a grade of 5.1 percent, and the second, the Telegraphe's 11.7 kilometers at 6.8 percent, Pantani unleashed himself on the big one. That was the Galibier, 18.3 kilometers at 6.8 percent to a height of 2,645 meters (8,728 feet).

Cheered on by an immense and soaked crowd, he left Ullrich, Julich, and their teammates planted. Four kilometers later, at the peak, he led them by 2:50.

Roaring through the descent with a group of early leaders, Pantani reached the start of the 8.8-kilometer climb, again on a 6.8 percent grade, to Les Deux Alpes with four companions. He travels fastest who travels alone, the Italian decided.

As the rain pelted down, Pantani pelted up. When he finally raised his arms in triumph as he crossed the finish line, he was 1:54 ahead of the next man, Massi, the nominal leader of the climbing competition.

Massi, who had collected points on the small hills that Pantani neglected, rode a brave race, but there was no confusion about who really was king of the mountains.

45. Stage 16: A Great Rider

JAN ULLRICH is a great Tour de France rider, as he proved in the 16th stage by storming away from all but one rival to win in the Alps. It was exactly the sort of dominating performance that could be expected of a man defending his championship in the Tour.

Unfortunately for Ullrich, the ride followed a rare off-day, in cold rain, in which he lost 8 minutes 57 seconds. Equally unfortunately, that one rival who managed to stay with him up and over the fearsome Madeleine Peak was Marco Pantani, the very man to whom Ullrich lost both the 8:57 and the yellow jersey the day before.

So Ullrich moved up from fourth place overall to third, and almost to second, but did not go far toward winning the race for the second successive year.

Pantani, on the other hand, moved closer to victory. By finishing second in a sprint finish, he widened his leadership to 5:42 over Bobby Julich in second place and 5:56 over Ullrich.

"The Tour de France is lost," Ullrich admitted after this 16th of 21 stages. "But my victory today was extremely important for me." He continued by praising Pantani's victory the day before as "incredible," considering the daylong cold rain that crushed Ullrich, a notorious summer soldier and sunshine patriot.

"I never expected him to race so well after the hard last week he had in the Giro," he said. "There's no doubt that he's the best mountain climber in the world."

With one day left in the Alps, where the Italian leader of Mercatone Uno had been outstanding, his big obstacle was the coming 52-kilometer (32-mile) individual race against the clock. Although such time trialing is not Pantani's strength, he was unlikely to lose a lead over five minutes.

That gap was obviously on Ullrich's mind when he accelerated away from a group of leaders with 14 kilometers to go on the Madeleine climb, 20.8 kilometers long with a grade of 7.6 percent. It is rated beyond category in difficulty, and followed four less-demanding climbs during the 204-kilometer trip from Vizille to Albertville.

Only Pantani was willing or able to follow him. As the overnight second- and third-place riders—Julich and Fernando Escartin, a Spaniard with Kelme—watched, Ullrich did all the work in the lead position, looking back constantly to see where the others were.

Except for Pantani, those others were soon out of sight. Within a few kilometers, the pair caught and left behind three riders from an early breakaway, including Ullrich's valiant teammate Rolf Aldag.

"In a climb like the Madeleine, I lose usually one minute every kilometer, so when we had more than five minutes' lead, I thought that gets me up five or six kilometers, and maybe I can help Jan if he goes," Aldag said. "I thought if he caught up to me on a flatter part of the climb, then maybe I can help him.

"The perfect thing would be to go over the climb and to help him in the valley. That would be perfect. But he caught me too far before that."

Aldag swerved over as Ullrich caught him and, with his face contorted by the effort, the domestique began to lead Ullrich. "It was just 300 meters or something, but at least it was good for his morale. I was suffering, sure. I was going 100 percent before and tried to do more for him.

"We made them work, the Mercatones. I think our big hope is to isolate Pantani from his team. It's so hard for Jan to drop him, but it's the only thing we can do. If we don't try anything, OK, the Tour's over."

Leaving Aldag behind, Ullrich and Pantani passed over the peak, 2:06 ahead, or enough to allow Ullrich to rise from fourth to second place.

Although the sun was out and the temperature balmy, the German did not repeat his error of the previous day, when he failed to bundle up adequately against the frigid wind on the descent. Then he wore only a lightweight jacket over his yellow jersey; this time he donned a heavier one. Pantani, more a traditionalist, jammed some newspaper pages into his jersey.

At speeds up to 85 kilometers an hour on the broadly curving 40-kilometer descent into Albertville, the two did their best to maintain their lead. Ullrich did about 75 percent of the work from the first attack until Pantani began taking his turn at the head, allowing his companion to rest in his slipstream.

They even jawed at each other as they rode side by side at one point, with Ullrich appearing to berate Pantani for lack of cooperation. The new man in the yellow jersey had much to gain by widening their lead: Even if it helped the German move up in the standings, he would gain no time on Pantani, but the Italian would gain on everybody else.

Behind them, Julich was riding with eight teammates and rivals, intent on guarding second place and slicing away at the gap.

"I didn't have a very good day today," the American said later. "I was suffering on the climbs and afraid of being dropped. But the cheering from the crowd kept pushing me on. I kept cramping badly [in the legs] in the last descent and could barely push the pedals for about five kilometers."

As the leading pair approached the finish, they broke into an unlikely sprint, the great puncher against the great climber. Neither one was Mario Cipollini, the king of the sprinters, but Ullrich was first by a few inches. In four stages in the Pyrenees and Alps, Pantani had won twice and finished second twice.

Julich finished third, 1:49 later, or enough to keep second place, with Escartin fourth and Axel Merckx fifth. Escartin dropped from third place overall to fourth.

The American was typically upbeat afterward. "The race isn't over until the time trial," he said. "Never say die." He was talking about winning the Tour, not about holding onto second place.

"Ullrich lost nine minutes yesterday and gained back two today," he pointed out. "Next time, maybe it will be Bobby Julich's time."

46. Stage 17: Time To Protest

THE TOUR de France was stopped twice during the 17th stage by rider protests and faced a premature end for the first time in its 95-year history.

The riders agreed to start the next morning only if the French police modified their tactics in the spreading investigation of some of the 21 teams. Not until Tour director Jean-Marie Leblanc consulted with government officials and promised a change in police methods—including questioning in team hotels rather than police stations—did the riders call off the second sitdown.

But they ripped off their numbers, making the stage unofficial, and then rode at a moderate speed without competition, reaching the finish line nearly three hours late. Five teams quit in protest, as did a handful of individual riders.

The turmoil was unprecedented since 1904, when the second edition of the race was almost the last because of cheating. Six teams were now under suspicion, the riders were divided in their response to the investigation, and Tour officials spent the day trying to keep the race going to its scheduled end.

The focus of the protest was a police raid on a hotel in which four riders from the TVM team were taken to a hospital the night before and tested for drugs in their urine, blood, and hair. "They treated us like criminals, like animals," said one of the Dutch team's members, Jeroen Blijlevens. "They took Bart out of the shower, made us sign some papers, and took us away," he continued, referring to his roommate, Bart Voskamp. The riders were held more than four hours for the tests and then released half an hour after midnight.

Word of their treatment did not reach the full 140-man pack until it was rolling in the 17th stage, 149 kilometers (92 miles) from Albertville in the Alps to Aix les Bains. The riders also learned then that the police would visit the hotels of three more teams, Casino, Polti, and ONCE.

As the news of the TVM treatment and the planned police investigation at the three team hotels that night filtered among the riders, they stopped for 25 minutes after 32 kilometers. "I'm fed up," said their spokesman, Laurent Jalabert. "I can't continue under these conditions, being treated like a criminal." He entered a team car, quitting the race, and was followed shortly by the other ONCE riders.

His directeur sportif, Manolo Saiz, a Spaniard, said: "We may never come to race in France again. This may be the end of cycling. It's the biggest crisis we've ever had, and we're a family heading for divorce."

Leblanc pleaded with the riders and their coaches to continue. "I ask you, directeurs sportifs, my friends, I ask you, the riders, my friends, to continue the race," he said on the radio that links the race.

"We were as astonished as the riders about the way TVM was treated," he said on television later. "We are discussing with the authorities how further investigation of the Tour de France riders can be handled with the utmost dignity."

With that promise, the race resumed, but only for a dozen more kilometers. Since Jalabert was gone, Leblanc met with the riders' new spokesman, Bjarne Riis.

"If the riders can be assured that the investigation will be held with a certain dignity, they will continue with the Tour de France tomorrow," Riis said.

The riders then resumed the journey at a speed about half their usual 40 kilometers an hour. At the feeding zone, the Banesto team, like ONCE from Spain, and the Riso Scotti team from Italy dropped out. So did individual riders, including two TVM riders. The Vitalicio team, and the Kelme team, both from Spain, announced later that they were withdrawing also.

By the end of the day, the field of 134 men was down to 101.

Although representatives of teams with riders among the leaders were not threatening further disruption, team officials and riders were outspoken in their condemnation of the police tactics. The police, who were acting under the orders of an investigating magistrate in Lille, far to the north, had no official spokesman and could not present their side.

"I understand the riders' unhappiness," said Alain Bondue, a former racer and now manager of the Cofidis team. "You have to let them do their job. The TVM riders left the hospital at 12:30 without eating and without being massaged. That's not right. That the police want to investigate is logical, but why not wait till Monday, a day after the race ends." Asked if Cofidis expected a visit from the police, he said, "Who knows? They don't telephone ahead."

The police were waiting at the hotels of ONCE, Polti, and Casino when the race finally pulled into Aix les Bains. The four TVM riders remaining, those taken to the hospital the night before, led the pack across the line and were applauded by a large crowd of fans who had stayed for that moment. Not all fans were so supportive: A few along the route jeered the riders and made obscene gestures using the large green cardboard hands that were distributed by a sponsor. The disgruntled fans ripped off all but the index finger, which they flapped at the pack.

"If the French police want to ruin their national race, they're doing it," said Bobby Julich. "We haven't been treated like human beings," he added. "Which TVM wasn't last night. That's what we're protesting against. That's why the stage was ruined today."

If the treatment continued, he said, "It was the understanding of the riders that it would have pretty dire consequences. That's pretty much what everyone said. Leblanc and Riis spoke; Leblanc said he spoke to the minister in charge of the police, he gave his handshake, he gave his word that nothing like last night would happen again."

Julich was crestfallen. "This was the stage I was waiting for," he said. "This was the stage where I was going to attack. I knew the place, the kilometer. And now the chance is wiped out. This was it—and now it isn't."

Other riders, who preferred not to be named, said they had been cool to the stoppages, but felt they had to concur in the mass action. "It just sort of came on after the start," said Kevin Livingston. "We'll see what happens tonight and tomorrow. It's just another time when you have to figure out what you want."

47. A Spectator's View

HIGH on the first climb in the Tour de France during the annulled 17th stage, Greg LeMond was waiting to watch the race go by and trying to understand why it was more than an hour behind schedule until he was told about the two stoppages by the riders.

"I believe they're protesting that it's gotten to be kind of a witch-hunt," said the American who won the Tour in 1986, 1989, and 1990. Now 37 years old and retired from the sport, LeMond was accompanying a 16-person tourist group that had been cycling over some of the Tour's roads before and after daily stages.

"The riders are trying to race the Tour de France," he continued in an interview. "You can't interrupt people's lives. The Tour de France is hard

American cycling legend Greg LeMond, now retired, chats next to an outdoor bar while attending the 1998 Tour as a visitor.

enough without interrupting people's lives. It's hard to say," he admitted. "I don't know the whole story. I'm an outsider now."

LeMond was critical of the French police, calling their raid on the TVM team's hotel in Albertville "an illegal search and seizure by American definitions. The riders feel they're being treated like dogs."

"But," he continued as he looked down the mountain and checked his watch, "this is probably good for cycling. It's a wake-up call. I think riders will think twice now about team-influenced programs. Drugs are the sick side of sports, not just cycling, but in many sports."

Doping problems, he said, were rare in his day. He first raced the Tour in 1984, finishing third, and last participated a decade later, when he had to drop out because of a weakness that was later diagnosed as a rare disease of his body cells.

"In the 1980s you could race totally clean, as I did," he said. "In the early '90s you started hearing things. But in the '80s, there was nothing like this, no. You heard about people taking steroids and most of the time they were caught. Now everybody believes everybody else is doing it. When some riders are flying, it creates intense pressures on riders and sponsors and teams.

"This is a terrible scandal. The reality is that to get everything out, they've got to figure ways to detect everything. It's sad for some of the riders, but they're the victims of a system that needs to be changed.

"Yes, you can say that a rider should resist the pressure to dope himself, but when it's some guy with a wife and a couple of kids who faces the loss of his job, or maybe his salary is going to drop from $10,000 a month to $3,000 because he has no results, then it's fair to call him a victim."

48. Stage 18: Time for Reflection

THE TOUR continued without incident the next day as the 101 remaining riders yielded to enormous pressure against aborting the bicycle race for the first time since it began in 1903.

After the riders staged two sitdown protests and threatened not to start if the police persisted in what were regarded as brutal methods of questioning riders in the widening drug scandal, the French police backed off. They did check four teams at their hotels after the finish and took a leading rider, a coach, and a team doctor into custody, but the racers decided that their rights had not been violated and set off the next morning.

Many teams with riders high in the overall standings and a chance at prestige and a share of the $2.2 million prize list were happy to keep racing until the end in Paris three days away. Other teams, like U.S. Postal Service, which is adamant against doping, remained "for the glory of the sport and because this is the focus of our entire season," as Dan Osipow, the team's director of operations, put it.

Another major factor in the continuation was that such firebrand teams as ONCE, led by Laurent Jalabert, had pulled out and were not participants in the discussion that the riders had as they rolled together at the start. Who knows, too, how many favors were called in by the organizers and how many deals struck by them with the directeurs sportifs of the 15 teams still in the race?

The rider taken into custody, Rodolfo Massi, the leader in the climbing competition, was still being held on suspicion of having a suitcase full of banned drugs, and so was Nicolas Terrados, the doctor for the ONCE team. The directeur sportif of the Française des Jeux team, Marc Madiot, was released too late to make the start.

Five teams withdrew before the start of the 18th stage, 218.5 kilometers (136 miles) from Aix les Bains, France, to Neuchatel, Switzerland, as cowbells rang out to celebrate the racers' brief incursion. Crowds in France were more reserved, with spectators expressing disappointment over the annulled stage because of protests by the riders but not anger toward them.

In many conversations with fans, they voiced indifference to the doping scandal and cited the special role that the Tour has in French life and culture. All along the French part of the route, for example, parents and grandparents held small children in their arms and began pointing and talking excitedly to them when the race approached.

The scandal over illegal performance-enhancing drugs, which originally concerned only the Festina team, then spread to TVM, had now spread to Big Mat-Auber from France and the four teams whose hotels had been searched the night before: ONCE, Casino, La Française des Jeux, and Polti.

Nevertheless, the race continued for most riders, even if the remaining TVM men dropped out; they were weary and without motivation, some said, but the cynical said they were determined not to return to France and further questioning.

In sunny and hot weather, the winner of a mass sprint once again was Tom Steels. Erik Zabel was second and Stuart O'Grady third. They, and 42 other members of the pack, finished in 4 hours 53 minutes 27 seconds, a speed above 44 kilometers an hour.

Marco Pantani continued to wear the leader's yellow jersey by 5:42 over Bobby Julich and by 5:56 over Jan Ullrich. The previous fourth-placed rider, the Spaniard Fernando Escartin was stricken from the rolls when his team joined the three others from Spain and withdrew. Massi, the king of the mountains, had been in seventh place overall when he was taken away.

Over their breakfasts of pasta mixed with eggs and wheat germ, Julich and Kevin Livingston talked of their feelings about the conduct of the race, confessing anger, sorrow, and confusion.

"Guilty by association is not the correct way of doing things," Julich said. "Just because a friend of yours steals a car doesn't mean that you're a car thief. The problem here is being publicly ridiculed and physically violated by the police."

He and Livingston both worried about the reaction in the United States to the doping reports. American riders are known for their aversion to illegal drugs. "But this is a sport where we're constantly pushing ourselves to the limit and vitamins and daily recuperation are a must," Julich pointed out. "That's why our doctors are here. There's no reason other than that. It's a tough sport that we do, 200 kilometers a day, day after day, and recovery is important."

Livingston said that he worried about confusion over the scandal. "Not too many people understand what's going on, including us. But if it goes on like this, there won't be any sport. It can't go on like this."

Julich agreed. "We're killing the sport in the most beautiful race in the world," he said. "Riders like myself have peaked their season around this three-week period. For all this to happen now takes away from all the hard work and sacrifices we've made."

As the second-placed rider, he also worried that if he stood on the one-two-three final victory podium in Paris, his triumph would be valid. "This is what I've worked for my whole career and it takes a little away when, 10 years down the line, you may see an asterisk by the result. I hope that isn't the case. I hope I've gained respect. If I do make the podium in Paris, I hope I'm able to smile when I'm up there.

"Then again," he said, "it's only a bike race. I was looking through the newspaper and on the page after all the stuff about the Tour de France, there's a picture of a starving kid in Sudan. That makes you realize,'Hey, man, this all has to be taken in perspective. There are a lot bigger problems in the world.'"

49. Stage 19:
The Longest Day

FRANKIE ANDREU said before the start of the 19th stage that his legs were dead and that there was no point in expecting him to join a large, early breakaway. "No way," he said. "No legs."

Andreu sounded convincing even though his goal in this Tour, his seventh, was identical with his goal in the first six: Get in a good breakaway and win a stage. It had not happened yet and there were only three days to go before the finish.

A breakaway was expected by nearly all the 96 riders left, since the journey from La Chaux de Fonds in Switzerland to Autun in France

Stefano Zanini's son wears the polka-dot jersey his dad wore briefly during the early stages of the Tour. He is greeted by fellow Italian polka-dot wearer Rodolfo Massi.

measured 242 kilometers (150 miles) and most teams with top sprinters, like Mapei and Telekom, let it be known that they were too tired to lead a long chase for a chance at a mass rush to the final line.

Moreover, all the leading riders would be expected to save themselves for the long individual time trial the next day. Since their teammates would be needed to keep them out of trouble on this stage, that meant no Mercatone Uno or Cofidis riders in any chase. With only 14 of the original 21 teams left after the withdrawal of the last five TVM riders and at least four teams intent on a restful day, the road was open to an early acceleration.

Jacky Durand, an unwearying early attacker, made that acceleration seconds after the start. After bursts of counterattacks, he was joined by 12 other riders and the rest of the pack just waved good-bye.

Andreu was one of the 13 fugitives, of course. "I had to go," he said later. "There were all these early attacks and the team was covering them and this one was mine. This team is trying hard to win."

Although the major goal of U.S. Postal Service was to win a stage, the closest it had come so far was Tyler Hamilton's second place in the first time trial. It also had a third place, a fourth place, and two fifths in the first 18 stages.

The breakaway's lead rose quickly. By kilometer 35, well over the border into France, it was 2 minutes 15 seconds, and by kilometer 39 it was 4:30. Pursuit was lackadaisical: By kilometer 50, as the riders passed a long line of brown cows marching to pasture, the lead was 6:40, and at kilometer 74, the start of a vast and sweet-smelling pine reserve, it was 14:05.

In two parallel lines, the 13 riders worked well together, taking turns in setting a fast pace at the front, slipping back in the file on the right and then mounting to the front again on the file on the left.

Andreu had a teammate in the attack, Pascal Deramé, a Frenchman, but there were also two riders each from Gan, Casino, and Big Mat-Auber, so that advantage was nullified.

The riders continued to work together, and their lead reached a peak of 17:30 just before they entered Burgundy and its long slopes of vineyards. On the only climb of the day, a small hill, Deramé bolted away from the 13 and was joined by Magnus Backstedt, a Swede with Gan; Maarten den Bakker, a Dutchman with Rabobank; and Eddy Mazzoleni, an Italian with Saeco.

The foursome's gap grew to perhaps 200 meters. With his teammate in front, Andreu remained put at the back of the second group. "I protected Pascal," he said. If he had worked with the chasers, he might have helped overtake Deramé. "He made a good move and looked strong. He had a good chance of winning."

With three kilometers to go and the foursome's lead at 18 seconds, Deramé accelerated on a left-hand curve. He managed to build a small gap but was overtaken with a kilometer and a half left.

Seeking that first stage victory for U.S. Postal Service, Deramé started the final sprint 200 meters from the line. Backstedt accelerated from fourth position and passed everybody else on the right, winning by a bicycle length. Den Bakker was second, Mazzoleni third, and Deramé fourth.

The Swede was timed in 5 hours 10 minutes 14 seconds, a speed of 46.8 kilometers an hour on a hot and sunny day. Eight of the nine others in the original breakaway finished 25 seconds behind, with the main pack 16:38 behind.

Since none of the 13 men in the attack ranked high in the overall standings, nothing changed at or near the top. Marco Pantani remained in the yellow jersey, 5:42 ahead of Bobby Julich and 5:56 ahead of Jan Ullrich. While Pantani is not usually a strong time trialer, his lead was so large that he was not expected to be overthrown the next day on the 52-kilometer course.

When the stage into Autun was over, Andreu had no regrets. "I couldn't chase after Deramé, my teammate," he said. "But if we caught them, I would be on my own and planned to attack myself, going for the victory. I thought I had a chance in the sprint.

"That's cycling," he concluded. "We rode a good race, it didn't work out, but maybe it will next time."

50. Stage 20:
His Own Merckx

AS OEDIPUS learned in Thebes and Wilhelm Friedemann Bach in Saxony, it's not always a smart thing to go into the family business. No matter how sweet a sarabande or rousing a crescendo the first son of Johann Sebastian Bach composed, there was always somebody around to tell him that it didn't come close to his father's Fifth Brandenburg Concerto.

Axel Merckx knows the feeling. A week short of his 26th birthday, the Belgian was riding in his first Tour de France. At that age, his father had already won the Tour three times, including his debut in 1969. Eddy Merckx

Axel Merckx shows some surprise when he is asked to sign a copy of a book devoted to his father, the legendary Eddy Merckx.

went on to win the Tour five times and share the record with Jacques Anquetil, Bernard Hinault, and Miguel Indurain.

They were all giants, and Axel Merckx was the first to admit that he was not. "I'm me, not my father," he said irritably. "Almost nobody gives me the chance to be myself." He also did not appreciate questions early in the Tour about whether he hoped to win it, or even a stage, in his first attempt. "I'm simply trying to be a good rider." His father won more than 400 races and the son had won two.

Nevertheless, the younger Merckx, who rode for the Polti team from Italy, had performed well enough to find himself in 11th place among the 96 riders remaining before the 52-kilometer (32-mile) individual time trial in Burgundy from Montceau les Mines to Le Creusot. A speedy race against the clock could put him into the top ten, a heady achievement and most riders' dream.

Snarling his way through some tricky curves to the finish line, the mild-mannered Merckx did it. He finished ninth for the day, failing by 4 seconds to overtake the rider in 10th place overall, but moving into the elite when the eighth-placed rider, Bjarne Riis, had a bad day and dropped to 11th.

Merckx was not the only man moving up on the rainswept, undulating course. Jan Ullrich, the master of the time trial, made up the 14 seconds by which he trailed Bobby Julich and rose to second place overall.

Both riders, being realists, thought they had no chance of catching Marco Pantani, who wore the yellow jersey by nearly 6 minutes. They were right. Ullrich won the race against the clock, in which riders started three minutes apart, in a time of 1 hour 3 minutes 52 seconds, a speed of 48.8 kilometers an hour. Julich finished second, 1:01 behind, as he dropped to third place. Pantani was third, 2:35 down, and, barring accident, was assured of victory by 3:21 overall when the race ended with a mainly ceremonial stage into Paris the next day.

Asked how he felt about losing second place overall, Julich said, "I lost nothing today. I won third place. I'm very, very happy to mount the podium with Marco Pantani and Jan Ullrich." Ullrich was first the year before, Pantani third, and Julich 17th.

Merckx was targeting a lesser man, Giuseppe di Grande, an Italian with Mapei, who held 10th place entering the 20th of 21 stages. If 4 seconds separated them at nightfall, 1 minute 2 seconds had been the gap in the morning.

"I'm hopeful," Merckx said beforehand. "One day at a time."

Afterward he was pleased. "I wanted to finish 10th, and it's done," he said. "I wanted to grow up in this Tour, and it's done. I wanted to go fast and I did."

The Tour, he felt, was harder than the Giro d'Italia, which he rode in May and June. "The Tour is faster, more nervous in the first half," he said. "I'm not familiar with this level of pressure, which calls for so much energy." He explained that his memories of his father's Tour victories were dim. "I was six when he stopped racing. I only know of the unbelievable things in his career from listening to his stories and watching videotapes.

"I understand that I'll never be as good as he was, but frankly it doesn't bother me. Since my career started, the media have compared me to my father. I remember how many journalists came to my 11th race because they all expected me to win that day, as my father did for the first time when he rode his 11th race. It was ridiculous."

Even if he had rarely won as a member of the Telekom, Motorola, and Polti teams, the younger Merckx had such fine results as third in the 1996 Tour of Lombardy one-day classic and fourth that year in the world championship road race.

"That fourth place has had a bad influence on my career," he said. "Since then expectations about me have been too high. People expected much more than I could deliver then."

Now he was starting to fulfill expectations, including his own. In an interview at the halfway point of the three-week race, he thought he would improve his position, then 37th overall.

"I feel good," he said. "Normally I'm always better toward the end, a week and a half from the finish, the last week. So I'm waiting." He came on strong in the Alps, 11th in the first day there, fifth the next.

"He's a serious and steady rider who does best when the race is hardest," said Merckx's coach with Polti, Gianluigi Stanga. Another testimonial came from a boyhood friend, Tom Steels, then the Belgian national champion and the winner, in the Mapei team jersey, of three stages so far in the 85th Tour. "If the Tour lasted five weeks, Axel could win it," Steels said. "That's how tough he is."

Eddy Merckx was a somewhat tougher judge. "He's not doing badly," said the father early in the Tour. "It can be better, but it's the beginning for him. I hope he can do better in the Alps."

With the Alps past, Eddy Merckx sounded happier. "He did fine, Axel," he said. "Now comes the time trial. It's difficult for him, carrying the name. But Axel is doing what he likes to do and for me, if Axel's happy, I'm also happy."

51. Stage 21: Homecoming

A DEPLETED and demoralized Tour de France reached its finish in Paris in what riders, officials and observers agreed was a state of crisis for the world's greatest bicycle race and the sport itself.

Their consensus was that the drug scandal that enveloped the three-week race even before it began in Dublin on July 11 had devalued a national icon and would possibly alter the 95-year-old Tour forever. The scandal had also diminished the afterglow of France's triumph a month before in the soccer World Cup. Instead of a second high, the nation had been confronted by spreading gloom from an unexpected source—its beloved race. The Tour holds a special place in France's heart, attracting an

A happy and relieved Mercatone-Uno team waits its turn before the final honorary lap around the Champs-Elysées at the conclusion of the Tour.

estimated total of 15 million spectators, most of them families, to its roads annually. A billion more are said to watch on global television.

"You can't destroy a myth," insisted Jean-Claude Killy, the 1968 Olympic ski champion who was now president of the Société du Tour de France, the organizers. Nevertheless, there was talk already of a boycott of the 1999 edition by foreign teams, with the Spaniards leading the way. Four Spanish teams and an Italian one had quit the race to protest what they regarded as violation of human rights by police investigating the use of illicit performance-enhancing drugs.

The scandal, which was believed to be far from over, overwhelmed the athletic side of the race. Marco Pantani, who became the first Italian in 33 years to win the Tour after he dominated his rivals in the Pyrenees and the Alps, was consistently forced off front pages by news of drug raids and rider protests.

There was some wonderful racing, including what will become a legendary stage in the rainy and foggy Alps in which Pantani crushed his main rival, Jan Ullrich, the defending champion. But who will remember it? As Bobby Julich, the American who finished third behind Pantani and Ullrich, said, "10 years down the line you may see an asterisk" next to his result.

The riders deserved better, especially Pantani, who accomplished the rare double victory in the Giro d'Italia and the Tour de France two months apart; Julich, who became the first American since Greg LeMond in 1990 to mount the final one-two-three victory podium; and Tom Steels, the Belgian sprinter who won his fourth stage in the race on its final day.

But they were pushed aside by the unprecedented turmoil, which included the expulsion of the world's top-ranked team, Festina from France, after its directeur sportif said that he had supplied his riders with drugs. In all, two dozen riders, coaches, team doctors, and masseurs had been brought in for judicial questioning, and a quarter of them had been charged. Five Festina riders had admitted that they practiced doping with EPO, and the TVM team from the Netherlands was due in a French court the next day to testify in a parallel case.

Besides those two teams, members of two others had been taken into custody, and suspicion has fallen on two more in the Tour's 21 teams. A leading rider, Rodolfo Massi, the former best climber, had been arrested, and more Festina riders would be heard in court shortly.

The 96 riders remaining, less than half of the 198 who started, were the smallest total since 1983, when 88 finished what 140 began. The overall mood on the final day was somber, with little of the rider skylarking en route that usually accompanies the last of 21 daily stages. This time few mugged for the television cameras, wore a hat snatched from a fan or rode backward on their saddles.

The atmosphere was summed up by Frankie Andreu, who said he had been talking a few days before with Patrick Jonker, a Dutchman with Rabobank. "He said that when he came onto the Champs-Elysées this year, he wouldn't have the same kind of tingling sensation of 'I finished the Tour and accomplished something.' It's more like 'We made it to the Champs-Elysées, and now we can get out of here and be done with the race,'" said Andreu, who finished all seven of the Tours he had ridden.

Jean-Marie Leblanc, the director of the race, echoed the feeling. Asked if he was happy that the race had continued despite two strikes by riders and a threat by them to go home before the finish, he said, "Happy? I'm happy only to reach Paris. Otherwise I'm not happy."

Fan reaction was difficult to gauge, since heavy rains nearly every other day reduced the number of spectators, a fact that could not be laid to indifference. At the finish, the Champs-Elysées seemed as crowded as usual, despite more rain and the start that weekend of the nation's four-week summer vacation.

For many, the Tour was still the Tour, a highpoint of the summer, and they were quick to dismiss the drug scandal.

Among such observers as former riders, however, the mood was more sober. Graham Jones, a Briton who finished three of his Tours, judged that the race and the sport were in a crisis, "the biggest that we've ever seen in cycling."

"Definitely a crisis," said Jean-Claude Leclercq, a former French national champion who rode five Tours and now worked for Swiss television. "A crisis and an embarrassment," said Marino Lejaretta, a Spaniard who rode eight Tours and now worked for Eurovision.

"A pity, a shame, a crisis for all of us," said Eddy Merckx, the Belgian champion who won the Tour five times and was with the race to watch his son, Axel, finish 10th overall.

Stephen Roche, the Irishman who won the race in 1988 and played a leading role at the start in Dublin, called this "a very rough time" but thought "some good has to come out of it. Everybody admits there's a problem and that cycling has to get its act together," he continued. "That's a good place to begin."

The unanimity cracked when questions were raised about who was to lead the investigation into the use of illegal drugs. Few riders and officials believed in the International Cycling Union, whose president, Hein Verbruggen, spent the last tumultuous half of the Tour on vacation and the first half at a conference.

Fewer still trusted in the efficiency of the many panels that would be set up or in the government officials who promised tighter laws on drugging.

"From past roundtables and conferences, I'd say nothing's going to happen," Andreu said in a typical comment. "It's so political, and it's always the same guys involved and they want to stay in power. That's their political agenda."

With their broad investigative power and sophisticated laboratories, the police and the courts appeared to many to be the only credible alternative.

"The sport will go on," said Mark Gorski, general manager of the U.S. Postal Service team. "They'll clean out whatever elements need to be cleaned out. If it's taken the French police to do it, then that's what it took."

PART III:

ALONG
THE ROAD
OF THE TOUR

52. A Furtive Outsider

H E HAD a furtive look, which set him apart from the other people in the pressroom. The others looked bored, happy, busy, or any combination of these, but not furtive—they belonged. The green card with an individual photograph that hung on their chests said so. The fellow with the furtive look had no green card.

Then how did he get past the two guards at the door and into the pressroom? No problem there: Lots of people do it. They like to take photographs of reporters at work, popping bright lights into their eyes. Then they look uncomprehending when a reporter asks if he can visit their grocery or shoe store some afternoon and stare at them, maybe even take photographs while they try to work.

There are also people in the pressroom who do have the proper accreditation, that green card, but have never been known to write an article. Didier, the super fan, is one of them. He shows up at every Tour, and many other big bicycle races, struts a bit, and never misses a buffet table. He represents a press agency named for himself and no doubt based in his living room, good enough for whoever issues press credentials.

Unlike Didier, the furtive fellow did not strut. He was too old for that—at least early 50s—and too heavyset. He looked hunted. His eyes were never still, as if he was searching for the one person among the hundreds in the pressroom who would betray him to the authorities and cause him to be evicted.

Until then, he showed up in the pressroom day after day wherever the race traveled. He seemed to be carrying more too, all of it clutched tightly to his body: In Rouen, at the start of the 1997 Tour, a black briefcase; by Pau, midway through, a couple of filled Tour plastic bags joined the briefcase. He gave the impression of a man fleeing a fire with all his possessions.

Everybody else needed a pass, but he circulated in the by-invitation-only area before each day's stage and waited at the fenced-off finish line afterward. At the long time trial in St. Etienne, where the riders set off individually to race the clock, he collected autographs from dozens of them, crossing the barriers with impunity to chat with riders as they warmed up on rollers. He took photographs, using the kind of camera that gets turned in at the developer's.

It got to be too much, a few reporters felt. Generally they don't like super fans, believing that even if they do no real harm and never get in the way, they burlesque the seriousness of the job. (If that sounds pompous, it is.) Near the end of the three-week race, some of those reporters discussed the furtive man and whether he should be turned in and barred from the pressroom, the finish line, the warm-up area, and all the other places where only people with the right papers could go. No decision was made.

The furtive man was around for the last stage, of course, the one on the Champs-Elysées in Paris. Once the riders sprinted across the final line and took their team's lap of honor, they all headed for a nearby hotel, and so did he. This time he was clutching not only the briefcase and the plastic bags and his camera and a notepad for autographs, but also the hand of a boy in his early teenage years. The boy had thick glasses, a vacant stare and a heavy way of walking, as if he was dragging his thick legs, not striding.

His father was pointing out riders to his son, walking hand in hand to where they were getting off their bicycles, calling them by their first names and introducing the boy. He had spent his Tour making friends, and now he wanted them to meet his son. No reason to be furtive about that, is there?

53. The Man in the Yellow Jersey

MARCO PANTANI returned home to Italy to more than a hero's welcome after his victory in the Tour de France. He was acclaimed *campionissimo*—champion of champions, a title that is not easily earned.

The last authentic one was the fabled Fausto Coppi, the winner of the Tour de France in 1949 and 1952; the winner of the Giro d'Italia, the world's second-ranked bicycle race to everybody except Italians, in 1940, 1947, 1950, 1952, and 1953; the world road race champion in 1953; the Italian national champion in 1942, 1947, 1952, and 1955; the record holder for the hour's race against the clock in 1942; and the winner of every major Italian one-day classic and then some.

That was pretty swift company, but Pantani won his right to be included. The 28-year-old leader of the Mercatone Uno team was the first Italian in 33 years to win the Tour de France. He was also the first man since Miguel Indurain in 1993 to win both the Giro and the Tour in the same year. The only other riders to have done it were the big stars: Coppi, Jacques Anquetil, Eddy Merckx, Bernard Hinault, and Stephen Roche.

"He's a throwback, the old-fashioned kind of rider," said Prime Minister Romano Prodi of Italy in a phone interview. Prodi, a big fan of professional racing and the riding companion of such Italian stars as Gianni Bugno, meant that Pantani did not base his season on one major race. "A real star," he said. "It's unbelievable what he's gone through, the sacrifices and pain he's known."

The charismatic Pantani was hit by a car going the wrong way in the minor Milan–Turin race late in 1995, fracturing his left leg. He spent the rest of that season, and most of 1996, on crutches, learning to walk again. In 1997 he had recovered well enough to finish third in the Tour, the same placing that he had in 1994. But bad luck struck him again in the Giro in June 1997, when a black cat—yes, really—crossed the road and caused a mass crash as riders tried to swerve around it. Pantani went down and was out until the Tour a month later.

In 1998, though, all went right. He won the Giro by dominating his opponents in the mountains, just as he did in the Tour, and then riding a superlative time trial, finishing third.

Acknowledged to be the sport's swiftest climber, the 1.7-meter (5-foot-7-inch), 60-kilogram (132-pound) Italian came into the Tour with many complaints: The mountains were not difficult enough, he said, and only two of the five daily stages in the Pyrenees and Alps ended on a peak, depriving his rivals of the chance to catch him on long descents. Nevertheless, he finished second and first in the Pyrenees and first and second in the Alps. The final Alpine stage was canceled by a riders' protest.

With a lead nearing six minutes before the final time trial, he again finished a surprising third, guaranteeing himself victory by 3 minutes 21 seconds when the Tour ended. That was margin enough to subdue panic when he had a flat on one of the first of 10 laps on the Champs-Elysées and had to be rushed back by his teammates to the main pack.

But Pantani rarely gives in to panic. "His biggest virtue is his intelligence," said Felice Gimondi, the last Italian until Pantani to win the Tour. "He has an acute sense of the race."

Pantani, who used to be known as Il Elefantino, the Elephant, because of his Dumbo-like ears, had reshaped his image in the last few years. Now he preferred to be known as Il Pirata, the Pirate, with his ears hidden

After the 1998 Tour, Marco Pantani, shown here shortly before the finish on the Champs Elysées in Paris, went home to a hero's welcome in Italy.

under a bandana, his head shaved, an earring in his left ear, and a suave moustache and goatee.

For some reason, possibly to blend with his yellow jersey, he had his black facial hair dyed blonde for his appearance atop the final victory podium.

As he said, his beard will have to turn gray before he also attempts to compete in the sport's third major stage race, the Vuelta à España. Not even throwbacks still ride the three big races in one year. Nor did he plan to appear in the post-Tour criteriums, basically exhibition races. Instead, said his father, Pantani would spend some time at home in Cesenatico, on the Adriatic in Emilia-Romagna, working in the garden and relaxing.

Otherwise his future was golden. He had an offer to move from Mercatone Uno to the Mapei team in Italy at a salary reported to be above $2 million annually, but rejected it. Loyal to his employers, Pantani was still marked by all the sacrifice and pain.

"I'm proud to have suffered for cycling," he said, admitting that he had only one unsettling moment in the Tour. "That was when I fell in the descent from the Aubisque," the first of four major climbs on the first day in the Pyrenees. "My hands were frozen and I had almost no feeling in the tips of my fingers. But the fear of losing wasn't in vain, because it caused me to react, to take nothing for granted."

He arose from that fall, got back on his bicycle, and finished second. The next day, in the mountains again, he won. He had started to construct his overall victory.

54. Jaja's Last Stand

SUN saturated the start village of stage 17 in Albertville. This was not one of the Tour's picturesque starts—one thoughtfully placed in a quaint town center, one which harked back to a bygone era. No, the Albertville start was set out on a nondescript parking lot on the edge of town. And this was not the friendly sun of France's Midi region, or even better, that of Provence. Albertville's sun produced a harsh glare effect that bleached the colors of clothes and rendered skin tones bland. A nice day, made less nice by its surroundings.

Laurent Jalabert was doing his best to stay clear of the violent rays; the 149 kilometers which awaited him on the day's stage would offer "Jaja" plenty of time to work on his tan lines. Instead Jalabert found shade under one of the many parasols offered at the various VIP areas in the village. And it was here where the world's number-one-ranked rider held his daily court.

Around him were the usual lines of fans and journalists. Jalabert, you see, is never at a loss for attention. Down-time is a rarity. But this year is particular. Just in case he didn't already garner enough attention, he is now wearing the distinctive tri-colored blue-white-red jersey of the French national champion.

Only a week prior to the start of the Tour, he finally succeeded in grabbing one of the few titles that until then had still eluded him. As a member of the Spanish ONCE team, Jalabert has always been troubled by the French championships. He has no other French teammates and thus invariably finds himself isolated against his countrymen, most of whom ride for top domestic teams, such as Gan, Casino, and Festina.

The 1998 circuit in Charade, however, was one of the toughest in history; thus, teammates were of little use. It turned out to be a classic race of attrition, and Jalabert showed that—among his countrymen at least—he was the strongest in such a race.

But despite his most recent success, this year's Tour had turned sour for Jalabert. And although he was clearly unaware as he chatted before the start, his Tour would soon end.

Across the village, riders of the Dutch TVM team cloistered together. Only last night several of their members were arraigned by police in the latest doping chapter of the Tour. Met by the authorities after the stage, they were immediately taken to the local police station before they had a chance to shower, eat, or receive the traditional massage. The peloton was only becoming aware of their demoralizing experience. But it would soon cripple another Tour stage.

In addition to the onslaught of doping scandals ravaging the race, however, Jalabert's own performance was suffering. About the doping scandals, he remained tight-lipped. He was only talking about the racing now.

After the Tour's rest day in the town of Tarascon, Jalabert led a sit-down strike with the Tour cyclists protesting the way in which the riders were being treated by the press as well as the police. But when certain teams broke rank and resumed racing, Jalabert was outraged.

He chased back through the pack, and with the help of his brother Nicolas on the Cofidis team and TVM.'s Bart Voskomp, Jalabert took off on an uncanny, near suicidal attack. For a rider in the top five overall, this day should have been a transition stage—a day to save energy, not waste it.

But Jalabert's move was his way of responding to teams like Telekom. In his eyes, their desire to race revealed his German rivals to be little more than a bunch of strike-breakers. "If you boys are so keen to race," he seemed to say with his vicious attack, "I'll make you race harder than you could ever have dreamed today."

Jalabert, however, paid for his heroics when he cracked in the Alps. His symbolic break with his brother seemed ill-timed at best. For many it was simply frivolous, obviously not the best preparation before the second wave of mountains in the Tour. And when Jalabert cracks, he cracks hard. Fifteen minutes, thirty-three seconds was his deficit to Marco Pantani on stage 15 to Deux Alpes, and over eight minutes separated him from Jan Ullrich on stage 16 into Albertville.

Also shying from the sun on this morning in Albertville was American rider Kevin Livingston. He was 100 meters clear of the start village where Jalabert sat talking. The day before, however, Livingston was next to Jalabert at the front on the Madeleine pass when the Frenchman folded. "He was right there and then boom!" explained Livingston. "It is so strange. Laurent is so powerful and he rides so effortlessly. One moment he can really be putting the hurt on you. Then suddenly, nothing."

"Yeh, that's what a lot of guys say," Jalabert responds when he hears of Livingston's remark. "I guess I'm the only one that is not surprised when I blow. I guess I hide my cards well. But I know when I'm on the edge. I know when my number is up." Jalabert smiles as he describes his weakness.

Despite his reputation as one of the world's most consistent winners, Jalabert is still susceptible to the bonk—that empty zone cyclists reach when their body's reserves are running on empty. It is something that he has faced on numerous occasions throughout his career. His first big bonk came in the 1992 Wincanton Classic. After leaving the field with Italian rider Massimo Ghirotto, Jalabert—the superior sprinter—was expected to handle the Italian veteran. Instead, he faded in the final kilometers and had to settle for second.

Since his professional debut in 1988 with the Toshiba team, Jalabert has been touted as the country's best cycling talent since… well, Bernard Hinault. Sure Hinault was firstly known as a Tour rider, and Jalabert is firstly considered a classics rider. But since no countryman seems able to win the Tour these days, the French can't be too picky about their champions. Besides, Jalabert has given them plenty to cheer about these last ten years with victories in prestigious classics like Milan–San Remo, Flèche–Wallonne, and the Tour of Lombardy, as well as stage races such as Paris–Nice and the Vuelta à España—the Tour of Spain.

Yet scattered throughout his many successes have been blatant collapses. Wincanton was the first. But there have been others. He was the heavy favorite in the 1997 Tour of Flanders. For much of the legendary Flemish race he was on the front, leading the attacks. Then strangely, 31 kilometers from the finish, he folded. Later that year he also lost the Vuelta à España when he ran out of gas five kilometers from the top of the Sierra Nevada climb on stage seven, the same stage, ironically, that he dominated in 1995.

If bicycle racing teaches one thing, however, it is knowing one's limits. The most successful riders learn their limits, accept them, and ride within them. For the most part, Jalabert understands this principle and doesn't try to defy it. His salt-of-the-earth upbringing in small-town southern France has taught him that much. Jalabert knows he enters the danger zone whenever daily racing exceeds 200 kilometers or climbs near the 2,000 meter mark. And most of the time, when his body puts on the hazard lights, he relinquishes with little regret.

Defeat in the Tour de France, however, is another matter. And it is one he never takes lightly. This year in particular has provided Jalabert with a bitter reminder. "You know, the last couple of days have taught me one thing. I mean, I always knew it wouldn't be easy to win the Tour. But this year I really focused all my attention on this race. There was always a chance that under the right circumstances…" His voice trails off and he reflects behind his protective mirrored sunglasses.

Only with a journalist's persistence does he admit what is for a French cyclist of his caliber nearly inadmissible. "I'll never win the Tour de France. I'm just not strong enough. And that's tough to take. To know that the biggest race in the world, the one I most wanted to win, is the one I will never win."

Nevertheless, he tries to hold out some hope for today's stage from Albertville to Aix-les-Bains. The 149 kilometers are definitely within his range, as are the two major climbs. The Crêt de Chatillon climb has a maximum altitude of 1,635 meters and the final climb, the Col du Revard, tops out at 1,448 meters. No, on paper this stage has Jalabert's name on it. But the French rider is not optimistic. "Yeh, I think the stage is good for me, but with all of the fatigue I just don't know. You know, once you hit your limits you hit them.

"The Tour could last another 40 days and you'd still have the same guys on top. Or it could be a week shorter. It just doesn't matter. The competition at the Tour is so fierce that you quickly discover who is strongest."

The bell signaling the call to the start rings and Jalabert makes his way to the start, still answering questions as he rolls along. Just before reaching the line, he darts across to greet his brother Nicolas. The two joke easily as the final minutes are counted down. Another day of racing was about to begin, so it seemed.

But as the pack rolled out it slowly became evident that this would be no ordinary day in the saddle. What started as an easy ride fizzled altogether when the pack refused to contest the first bonus sprint. Then as they neared the first climb, they simply stopped.

Again a sit-down strike was called. Again various riders would state their cases. The riders were stung by stories of the TVM. police investigation. And with several additional teams now suspected of foul play, many felt that any rider on any team could suddenly be called in, little matter that they had a Tour de France to ride.

But this time, frustrated by the peloton's inability to organize under a common consensus, Jalabert abdicated his role as spokesman.

Been there, done that.

Instead, he opted for the passenger's seat next to his ONCE team manager Manolo Saiz. The Tour might continue, but without him.

Sure, Stage 17 could have been a good stage for the Frenchman. But instead, it turned out to be one stage too many. And quickly this Tour had become one Tour too many for the French champion. "Frankly I've had enough of this Tour. Everyone is free to make his own decision, but mine is made up from my heart and soul. I'm quitting this circus, this nightmare!"

Soon his entire ONCE team followed suit, and then all of the Spanish teams, plus the Italian Riso Scotti team. The Tour had never been nearer total collapse.

In the end, however, enough teams and enough riders decided they had enough interest that the Tour would finish in Paris. As Jalabert said, his decision was a personal one.

And likely his decision to pull out was motivated more by his own personal disappointments than his frustration with the manner in which French police and journalists were handling the doping affairs. After all, a few additional days of racing offered little chance for him to enhance his own performance.

After dropping out, he hit the beaches of Santander along Spain's northern coast with his family. His hibernation didn't end until the Saturday following the Tour, when he rode the San Sebastian World Cup classic.

But despite the break from the sport, he could still taste the bitter after-effects of this year's Tour. "If I have the choice, I'll never ride the Tour again," Jalabert told the French sports daily *L'Equipe*. "I put everything on the Tour this year. But this is my third year in a row of setbacks. Better to move on to other things."

For a French champion like Jalabert, such words are neither said nor taken lightly. But then Jalabert knows that the career of a champion is made up of victories, not defeats. He has already proved on more than a hundred occasions that he knows how to win races. And for "Jaja" at least, there are other races to win. The Tour, however, will surely not be one of them.

55. Tyler Hamilton's Quiet Fight

SOBBING, Richard Virenque exited Chez Gillou, a roadside tavern only meters from the finish of the first time trial in stage seven of the Tour de France. For the popular French star, his race was already over. After his Festina team was caught up in one of the ugliest drug scandals to ever hit the sport, Virenque and company were asked to leave the race.

Perhaps Virenque did not cry only for himself, though, but for all of France. After all, he has been touted as the country's best Tour hope in recent years.

But along the sinuous and hilly 58-kilometer time trial course in the Corréze region of central France, new riders were already giving the public fresh reason to cheer. Such is the irony of sport, and sports like cycling have built a long tradition on their ability to constantly provide new heroes.

Only moments before Virenque made his last stand, little-known American rider Tyler Hamilton, of the U.S. Postal Service team, had posted the best time of the day. And as more and more riders clocked their efforts, Hamilton's time held up. In the end, only defending Tour champion Jan Ullrich outrode the young American. Hamilton was clearly the hero of this day.

Sure, the French would have liked one of their own to grab the headlines to help them bury Virenque's blues. But in the end, cycling fans—unlike those in World Cup soccer—seem to know that their sport is one firstly of individuals. Nationality remains a detail reserved for the result columns. And that evening, as the results were finalized, plenty of people talking about "that Tyler Hamilton kid."

Hamilton, normally quiet, was stunned. "Honestly, I didn't expect that. Going into the stage, I would have been happy with a top 20, and here I am finishing in the top two." There was little apparent enthusiasm in his voice. Clearly Hamilton needed time to absorb the recent events which would forever change his professional cycling career.

Time trials, after all, are considered the race of truth. They don't lie. Only good legs and good lungs bring a rider a good performance. Hamilton's performance was a no-nonsense display of his true talent.

That evening, Hamilton was one of the guests of honor on the Tour talk show *Vélo Club*. He appeared as uneasy with the sudden stardom as he was with the French language. But fortunately his countryman Bobby Julich—who finished a solid third on the stage—was also an invited guest. Julich, who has had more experience handling the media, helped Hamilton put the performance in perspective. Speaking like a true American, he eyed Hamilton enviously and said, "Second place in a Tour de France time trial, that's worth a lot of money."

Suddenly the 27-year-old Hamilton was in fifth position overall in the Tour de France. Not bad for a virtual beginner in the race. Only a year ago, he was a Tour neophyte, a true debutante. With his Correze time trial he also showed that he was a fast learner. His stock was soaring. Immediately his U.S. Postal Service team director Johnny Weltz was talking about an eventual top ten performance.

Hamilton's stunning time trial represented yet another example of the blossoming second generation of English-speaking cycling stars. But while riders like Julich or Australia's Stuart O'Grady cite Greg LeMond and Phil Anderson as their childhood idols, Hamilton identifies more closely with Andy Hampsten. Ironically, they would become friends and roommates when they both rode for the Postal Service in 1996. "We

The American rider Tyler Hamilton provided one of the early surprises in the 1998 Tour de France with his second place in the stage 7 time trial. Shown here before the start of the 8th stage in Brive la-Gaillarde, he is cautiously optimistic.

roomed together a lot that year," Hamilton remembers fondly. "He taught me so much. And those old race stories, oh they were the best."

Certainly he was a natural-born time trialer. His first coach, Steve Pucci, remembers, "I first knew something was happening with Tyler when he won the New England district championship time trial in 1989 as a junior. He beat the senior riders, he beat everybody. And he was riding on junior gearing!"

But recently, Hamilton had raised more eyebrows as a climber. In Spain's Tour of Catalonia, just prior to the Tour, Hamilton was making the split with the top climbers over most of the mountains. Many insiders wagered that his combination of climbing and time trialing could make this second-year Tour rider one of the revelations of the race.

But what even a lot of insiders did not know, was that Hamilton had also been fighting against strange and unpredictable intestinal problems throughout the season. Only two days prior to the time trial, Hamilton was up all night with stomach problems. And up all night for Hamilton is not just about tossing and turning in one's sleep. It's about sitting on that porcelain throne, better know as the pot.

As a result, his body, depleted of any fuel, was running on empty, void of all force. "It is just on and off, totally unpredictable," explained Hamilton. "I've had a gazillion tests, and they all come out negative. But right now, it is the biggest hurdle in my career."

Only two days after the eye-opening time trial, Hamilton's rollercoaster Tour ride took another downward plunge. The evening after stage eight again saw him "up all night." And then stage nine was an unpleasant surprise—one of the hottest, longest days of the Tour. Dehydrated, physically empty, Hamilton finally fell off pace 40 kilometers from the finish into Pau.

Despite his third place position in the general classification, Weltz did not opt to send any riders back to help Hamilton through. Giving the young star up for dead, Weltz figured Hamilton would drop out, and any support riders would only risk finishing outside the time cutoff and thus be disqualified.

But Hamilton did finish. No, it wasn't pretty. His body, covered in goosebumps despite the 100-degree temperatures, had clearly shut down. "At the finish, it was like 'I can't believe what just happened to me.' That was definitely my toughest day as a cyclist. At one point Johnny [Weltz] told me it was my own call, but he didn't think finishing would be possible. And the team doctor drove beside me and told me I should call it."

So why didn't he listen to his advisors? "I guess I still had some fight left," Hamilton says without bragging. "Cycling has that way of bringing out your true sense of character. The highs are high and the lows are real low. I'd experienced them both in the space of just a couple of days, but I still wasn't ready to stop."

If stage nine was one of the hottest days of the Tour, stage ten was one of the coldest. The weather, like the Tour this year, was in a state of constant flux. Chilling rain and fog are hardly the weather most riders would order with legendary climbs such as the Aubisque, Tourmalet, Aspin, and Peyresourde, all on the day's menu.

Again, few expected Hamilton to finish. His bags went to the feed zone; a preventive measure for a rider expected to abandon. But again Hamilton surprised. "Frankly, I was psyched to see that rain. After that heat I was loving it. I just looked for the grupetto. And when I saw Eros Poli leading the caboose, I knew I was okay. When it comes to making the time cut-off in the mountains, Eros is the man."

Indeed, the six foot, three inch, 190-pound Poli is anything but a climber. So when the veteran Italian is not leading out sprints or chasing down breakaways, he often assumes the responsibility of getting the stragglers to the finish within the allotted cut-off time. And on the Tour's first mountain stage, Hamilton was only too happy to be one of those stragglers.

Over the ensuing days, Hamilton refound his fight. In the Alps, he even managed to attack. Like on stage ten in the Pyrenees, rain blanketed stage 15 from Grenoble to Deux Alpes. But remember, that's Hamilton's kind of weather. Already on the first climb, the Croix de Fer, he was part of an early attack. Then on the Galibier climb, when no more than 30 riders were still in the front group, he again accelerated.

It wasn't an attack that lasted long, nor one that garnered much attention. But it was Hamilton's quiet way of saying that he was still present, still accounted for. Other attacks soon followed. Frenchman Luc Leblanc countered first. And not so long after, Marco Pantani launched his memorable assault that would eventually win him the Tour.

Hamilton was far from the action by the time he finally reached the summit of the Galibier. But again he showed that he still had some fight in him. "I had to do something." explained the sober but stubborn rider after the finish. "I knew I wasn't going to make it over the top with the front. But if you're going to die, I figure it's better to die off the front, than off the back. I don't always live life that way. But sometimes it's just right."

56. Post-Tour Tummy Troubles

THE TOUR de France has been over for several weeks now. And Tyler Hamilton is back in his Massachusetts home of Brookline. Hamilton finished the Tour; something that fewer than a hundred other riders can claim this year. But less than three weeks later, Tyler's tummy troubles forced him to prematurely finish his season in Europe.

"I had salmonella poisoning," Hamilton seems almost happy to say, apparently relieved to have finally found a concrete cause for his intestinal ailments. And after three bedridden days in a Spanish hospital, he returned to the States to undergo further tests.

Johnny Weltz, his U.S. Postal Service director, however, is less upbeat. "Even though we were able to identify the problem this time, I think it is all linked to a greater problem we still don't understand. Tyler has been traveling with the team. He ate the exact same things everybody else ate, yet he was the only one to get sick. No, we've got to get to the root of this problem, otherwise Tyler will never be able to reach his full potential."

Hamilton is back living with Haven Parchinski, his fiancée. The Tour de France is only a memory, and despite the many frustrations he experienced this year, he is pleased with his own performance. "It is crazy to think that one day, one ride, really little more than one hour, could change my outlook on my cycling career so much. But it has," Hamilton reflects. "You know, it's not like I got second on some road stage after being in a lucky break with ten other guys. No, second in the first time trial, early in the Tour, when everybody—except Festina—still has fresh legs, is different. It gives me a lot of confidence for the future. I mean before the time trial, I always felt like I was capable of doing big things. But to be honest, I needed results to build up that confidence."

Another rider who has come to believe in Hamilton is his teammate Lance Armstrong. Only two years ago, Hamilton's eyes were filled with intimidation and admiration for the American legend as the two waited at the foot of podium in the Tour DuPont. As the overall race leader,

Armstrong was no stranger to the spotlight. Hamilton, however, was making a unique podium appearance after finishing third on the day. There was little communication between the two. Armstong, as always, was heavily solicited. And characteristically, Hamilton was content to simply look on and observe. Their careers had not yet crossed. But, like Andy Hampsten earlier, Armstrong has become teammates and friends with Hamilton.

"Whenever we're on the road, I try to room with Tyler. He's just one of those real likable guys," explains Armstrong. "And now, after his Tour de France, I'd really like to sit down and have a talk with him. That time trial he rode was no lie. That was a hot, hard, hilly course, a true strongman's course. But more importantly, Tyler is clearly not just some time trial monster. He's also a good climber. He could be the country's next top-ten Tour rider. So I would just like to see what he thinks he could do, to tell him what I think he could do, and to explain to him what the cycling community is going to expect of him now."

But despite the whirlwind of support stemming from his Tour de France performance, Hamilton does regret that his performance, like that of so many others in the '98 race, was persistently overshadowed by the flood of drug scandals. "I honestly had a hard time riding my bike after that. After the second protest day, it was simply hard to get on the bike. With all the scandals, the teams dropping out and all, the focus just wasn't on the race any more. And that was tough to swallow.

"I mean, I'd been training for this race all year. This is the only race I think about on a daily basis throughout the year. When I'm training in November and December in the cold, I'm already thinking about the Tour de France. Then something like this happens. It is just hard to race when your head isn't in it."

To see the Tour come under criminal investigation was hard enough for a young professional. But to see the illicit drugs some of his competitors were apparently taking was bewildering for someone like Hamilton, who still has his career in front of him. "It sucks that all this happened at the Tour de France, but we needed something like this to clean up the sport.

"The sport of cycling was getting, is getting, crazy with the drug problems. It's crazy to think about some of the junk that riders are putting into their bodies. To think all that stuff that was in the Festina team car was going to be in the riders' bodies by the end of the Tour. It was going to be all gone! No, the sport of cycling needs to get cleaned up, and after all of these events, it's going to be hard not to clean it up. I'm happy for that."

Nevertheless, Hamilton remains optimistic about the sport he has transformed into a career. "I know there are a lot more clean guys out there than people are saying. I know it is possible to be competitive in the Tour and be clean. There were a lot of new faces in this year's Tour. And maybe, with all of the drug scandals, the clean guys were finally coming to the top. And that gives us a lot of hope for the future."

57. Night in Jail

DRUG BUSTS are never pretty. Australia's Neil Stephens can vouch for that. Evicted from the Tour de France along with his teammates for supposed drug use, Stephens traveled from his home in Spain to the central French city of Lyon to answer questions regarding his potential involvement after his team director and team doctor admitted to systematic doping within the team.

But when he arrived, he quickly realized that this would not be a simple question-and-answer session. Accounts of what the riders like Stephens experienced in the hands of the authorities shocked many people involved in the Tour, as well as much of the general public. Clearly though, it served to demonstrate that the 1998 Tour de France was about much more than bike racing.

Here is one rider's story of his experience with the French legal system:

"You know, immediately after we left the Tour, I sought legal advice. My lawyers insisted that I didn't even have to go up to Lyon for questioning. I never received anything in writing or any phone call from the police requesting my presence. I just got a call from one of the team personnel. He said that, since I didn't have anything to hide, I might as well go and do the right thing.

"But that was never the case. It was not a simple questioning. As soon as we were in there, we were told it would be for 24 hours. And if they failed to get the information, they could hold us for up to four days.

"When I asked to see my lawyer they said no. I didn't have a right because I wasn't accused of anything. But then they say I could be held for four days. That's the way they treat a witness! No, the treatment was pretty barbaric. But for them [the police] it wasn't bad treatment perhaps. They're used to rapists and criminals and all.

"First I went through 11 hours straight questioning from 2 P.M. to 1 A.M. Then I was taken down and strip searched, told to bend over and they did the full body search thing. Finally I was given back some of my clothes, but not all.

"when I asked to have my shoes back so I could go urinate, they refused. The bathroom floor was covered in other people's urine, but I had no choice. I had to walk through it just to go to the bathroom. Plus in my cell, the names of other prisoners were written in feces. And I wasn't accused of anything!

"What they called a bed was about a foot and a half wide. I rolled up my pants to make a pillow. In the morning I was given a brioche that was about two or three days old. Ironically, the coffee was not too bad, actually. Obviously, that was all done to scare us. And the next day questions started again. When I finally said I couldn't give them any more information, they reminded me that I had only had one bad night. I could have three more if I didn't cooperate.

"Finally they did let me out. Officially, I admitted that I followed the treatment of my doctor. I had no way of knowing if I had been given any illegal substances. I certainly never agreed to that, or gave him permission to illegal substances. But still to this day, I don't know whether I was given anything illegal."

Pierre Masson, a Paris-based lawyer who works for the Franco-American firm Levine and Okoshken, puts Stephens' statements into perspective, "This is one of the foggiest aspects of French law. Neil, along with the other riders, was placed under what is known as 'garde a vue.' That is a concept that does not exist in many legal systems. Roughly, it means to be detained for questioning with suspicion of wrong-doing.

"In such a situation, a person may be held for a maximum of 24 hours with the possibility to extend, can make one phone call to a family member or an employer, may be examined by a doctor. And only after 20 hours, may the person see his or her lawyer confidentially, but for no longer than 30 minutes. It is a very delicate situation, because legally the person is still presumed innocent, but at the same time the person is suspected of being party to some wrong-doing. It is something that has come under a lot of scrutiny in recent years with the French people.

"Today, however, the law still stands as it is. As a result, I'm not surprised to hear about the way the riders were treated. The police obviously had some solid evidence, and they were going after it. They were playing hardball.

"What is positive is that riders like Neil were released before the end of the first period of 'garde a vue.' So provisionally, they were satisfied with his testimony and did not charge him with anything. That's a lot better than some of the other possible options the police had."

58. Drug Talk:
Taking Testa to the Limit

NOT ONLY cyclists abandon the Tour de France. Italian doctor Massimo Testa also dropped out. Already on the rest stage in Tarascon-sur-Ariege, Testa was getting, well, testy. That's when the France 2 television station went through the garbage cans of his Asics team hotel in an attempt to implicate his team in suspected drug use.

Found were syringes, as well as certain products which under certain circumstances could be prohibited. As they were found, however, they proved nothing. Nevertheless, with all of the tools known to investigative journalism, the fervent reporters implied guilt. Disgusted, he returned to his home in Como, Italy where he is a family doctor—most definitely a kinder, gentler way to make a living.

By Stage 16, he had had enough: enough scandal, enough police investigation, enough special reports by journalists concerning the prevalence of drug use in cycling.

"Sure I use cortisone with my cyclists. Sure I use intravenous injections. So what!" defended Testa. "That is legal. Heck, I use cortisone almost daily with my own patients back home. With cyclists, I use it particularly to combat allergies and knee problems. Quite often in a race like the Tour, things happen and cortisone is the only solution. When such things are used correctly and within their legal limits there is nothing wrong with that. As long as I present a prescription explaining the exact reason, the UCI authorizes such use, as does the Olympic Committee. It is only when it is abused that it poses a problem. What you can't do is use cortisone for any kind of systematic effect. You can't take cortisone pills or inject it into the veins.

"But at the Tour de France this year, the tables were turned," he continues. "There was so much confusion with everything, and I felt like the doctors were becoming the targets. I mean, the ONCE team doctor [Nicolas Terrados] was held by the gendarmes for 48 hours simply because they found some asthma products and other things doctors carry with them in case of emergencies—that is too much. We have to be able to practice our profession. In the end, I thought it was just best to leave." [The French sports daily *L'Equipe* reported that according to authorities, Terrados was held because certain unmarked bottles were found, as were certain doping products.]

Testa has served as a doctor on 13 Tours de France. And after working with Jim Ochowicz for over a decade on the 7-Eleven and Motorola teams, he now freelances for various European squads. But he is growing increasingly frustrated at the misperceptions of his profession within the sport. He understands that some of his colleagues are to blame.

The confessions of the Festina team doctor Eric Ryckaert concerning the systematic use of EPO on the French team disturbs Testa. "That is wrong," he says categorically. "A team doctor should never get involved in that. Our role is to monitor the athletes, to guarantee their health. And our job should stop there. It should never go beyond that. I refuse. Perhaps I'm naive. But I prefer that to being responsible for drug use in the peloton."

The cases of malpractice revealed in the Tour, however, have only confused the role of doctors in elite sports. Suddenly a simple hypodermic translates into doping.

For the record, top-level endurance athletes are no strangers to needles. Many vitamins and mineral supplements are administered in this manner simply because it is the most direct way for them to be absorbed by the body. These athletes are constantly submitting to blood tests as well as many other tests. Such a routine is necessary to detect deficiencies accrued in the body as a result of the grueling competition.

Clearly, however, the current crisis is about more than vitamin B12 supplements. But then, there is nothing new about drug use in cycling. Already in the 1924 Tour, the legendary Pélissier brothers—Henri and Françis—decried the wretched underbelly of the sport. After dropping out of the Tour, they revealed to Albert Londres, then a journalist for *Le Petit Parisien*:

"You want to see how we ride [The Tour de France]? Here… This is cocaine for the eyes, and chloroform for the gums… This is ointment to warm the knees. And pills? You want to see pills?"

They each pull out three containers.

"In short," said Francis, "We ride with dynamite."

Henri continues, "You haven't seen the showers at the finish? That's worth a trip. The stained mud, white like shrouds. The diarrhea empties us… And our toe nails, I have lost six of the ten. They just fall off progressively each stage. And you haven't seen anything yet. Just wait till we hit the Pyrenees. That's hard labor."

Londres entitled his soon-to-be-legendary story, "Les Forçats de la Route," or the slaves of the road. It shocked the sport, and it set a precedent that portrays the cyclists as victims.

Eventually though, the scoop of the century was shelved as an isolated case. The problem, however, is that it was not an isolated case. When rising French hope Roger Riviere crashed out of the 1960 Tour, paralyzed for life, amphetamines were found in his jersey pockets. Similar substances were found in the blood of British rider Tom Simpson when he collapsed from his bike on the Mt. Ventoux and died in 1967.

A decade later, French champion Bernard Thévénet was hospitalized after winning his second Tour de France in 1977. Later that winter, he admitted that cortisone abuse had rotted his liver. He was one of the lucky ones. He raced again, but never at the same level.

And in 1988, Spaniard Pedro Delgado was nearly suspended from the Tour while wearing the yellow jersey. Masking drugs were found in his body. Only a technicality allowed him to continue racing and win the Tour; at the time, the particular drug was banned by the Olympic Committee, but would not appear on the UCI list until after the Tour.

Until 1998, however, each of these situations was dismissed as an isolated instance, simply the evidence of bad eggs in the bunch. Until this year's Tour, the law of silence held truth hostage. Those who do talk only do so "off the record." But the numerous drug scandals that crippled the race revealed that indeed the drug problem was more prevalent than ever imagined. Or at least as dire as the most cynical skeptics predicted.

Clearly the temptation to take illicit performance-enhancing drugs is constant. But then it always has been. American champion Greg LeMond, who raced until 1994, remembers, "The problem is that everybody thinks everybody is doing it."

And quite obviously, cyclists are not the only tempted souls in sports. Since 1982, Bob Goldman, president of the National Academy of Sports Medicine, has surveyed Olympic-level American athletes concerning their views towards drug taking. According to the study, over 50 percent of 198 athletes surveyed in 1995 said they would take a banned substance that would enable them to win every competition for five years, then kill them.

No, these disturbing data are not something out of Ripley's *Believe It or Not*. Rather, it shows a true-blue, contemporary end-of-the-millennium nightmare all its own.

Despite the evolution and apparent increase of drug use in cycling today, Testa staunchly defends the idea that top riders can be both competitive and "clean." And even in 1998, when it became apparent that top teams could be implicated in drug abuse as easily as marginal ones, and that riders, as well as doctors, directors, and soigneurs were equally to blame, Testa remains optimistic. And even with the flood of drug scandals that hit the 1998 Tour, Testa still believes that a minority of cyclists in the peloton are actually involved in illegal drug use. Is Testa realistic, or simply idealistic?

Regardless of the supposed statistics, Testa insists, "I still have found nothing that proves to me that EPO or human growth hormones provide anything more than marginal benefits. They certainly wouldn't change the hierarchy of the sport. And that is something I try to teach my riders. There have been a few cases where I have suspected a rider," he admits. "But it is not my job to confront him about it. I can't go through his luggage looking for drugs. That would destroy the confidence they have in me. But what I can do is show them my files, show them all of the evidence I have collected on the subject, and try to convince them that doping is not worth it."

But a world of reason still doesn't halt the basic human instinct to get ahead. The current argument goes something like this: drugs are used increasingly in everyday life to reduce stress or minor aches and pains, so shouldn't elite cyclists—who suffer more than "normal" folks—at least be able to reduce their pain?

Cyrille Guimard, who has participated in nearly 30 Tours de France as a rider, team director, and sports commentator, presents another side of the problem. "You know, people have always looked to sports as a way to escape from the real world. We expect elite athletes to transcend everyday life with their performance. They are supposed to set an example. But now, what we have come to see, is that athletes and sports in general, is no different. It is simply a mirror of the real world, filled with many of the same vices."

The argument took on greater proportions when Juan Antonio Samaranch, president of the International Olympic Committee, suggested in an interview with *El Mundo* that performance-enhancing drugs needed to be re-evaluated, and those that did not pose a threat to the athlete's health should be removed from the list. "The actual list of [prohibited] products should be greatly reduced," Samaranch maintains. "Everything that doesn't act against the athlete's health, should not be prohibited." Testa disagrees: "That is very dangerous," he cautions. "today, we don't know what exactly is dangerous. And even if we manage to reduce the immediate risks of dangerous drugs like EPO, we still do not understand their potential long-term risks."

It is generally acknowledged that during the 1960s and 1970s, stimulants like amphetamines were the top choices for those interested in artificially improving their performance. Then as drug detection improved, the emphasis shifted to improving the amount of oxygen carried in the blood. Blood doping and transfusions replaced stimulants in the late 70s and 80s. EPO developed from such tendencies. Today, EPO appears to the base of current methods. But there is much talk about new products, such as human growth hormones and PFC (perfluorocarbon), what cyclists have horrifyingly nicknamed "death in a bottle." PFC is a product that binds oxygen and carries it through the blood, but also carries terrible risks.

In 1997, Testa was one of the key doctors who helped introduce blood testing among riders to monitor their hematocrit levels. Increased hematocrit levels are the most visible side-effects of EPO use, and today it is limited by the UCI at 50 percent. Skeptics claim that the tests actually legalize the use of EPO, so long as the rider's hematocrit level remains in check. Testa only shakes his head in bewilderment, "That certainly wasn't the intention of the tests. But until we find a way to actually detect EPO, these tests at least reduce the immediate risks."

Unfortunately, those trying to control drug use in professional sports always seem to be at least a half step behind those using it. It's an ongoing tug-of-war, one which those hoping to halt flagrant drug use may never win.

"You know it is impossible to test every athlete for every illegal substance," explained Anne-Marie Masson, anti-doping and medical coordinator for the UCI in 1997. "There are just too many drugs out there. It would be unrealistic." Instead, Masson explained that there is a certain hierarchy of substances tested. And only if the initial round of tests reveals something suspicious are further tests incurrred.

Yet despite the inefficiencies, Testa supports further tests. The UCI has proposed that every professional have a closely examined health file starting in 1998, with mandatory check-ups several times each season. It sounds confusing, even more bureaucracy for such apparently little benefit. But Testa supports the tests and defends their long-term benefit. "Rider files are the only way to establish parameters with each and every rider. That is the only way to determine if something is askew within an individual."

At the end of the 1998 Tour, Testa was as close as he had ever been to walking away from the sport. He was simply fed up with the direction the sport was going, and no longer knew if his role was a viable one. But after some time back in Como, time with his family, as well as his family clinic, he reckons he is ready to return to the sport.

"We've got a lot of work to do. Everybody in the sport has to sit down and try to figure out how we can seriously combat doping. And as for us doctors, we have re-establish what our role is in the sport. We have to make that clear, and be certain that we will be allowed to work under acceptable conditions." That may be asking a lot. But then Testa, don't forget, is an idealist.

59. Getting On: Festina Riders Reflect

I T IS a day Richard Virenque will likely never forget. And most likely neither will his Festina team or their many fans. "The day I had to leave the Tour, that was the hardest moment of this whole ordeal," remembers Virenque when he speaks of the drug scandal that saw his team expelled from the 1998 Tour de France.

Now though, nearly two months later, Virenque and company are making their "grand retour," their big return, to French bicycle racing at the Grand Prix Ouest France.

In the host town of Plouay, a small town nudged into the belly of the cycling-mad Brittany region, the recently humiliated riders are reunited with their fans.

But as conversations with Virenque and his Australian teammate Neil Stephens reveal, the effects of the "Festina Affair" on the various individuals within the team differ significantly.

At first glance, little has changed. Both riders are amiable. But as each one talks of the affair, neither can hide his unease.

Stephens is one of the first to arrive at the Novotel Hotel in nearby Lorient. He is happy to chat but is visibly distraught when he recalls his recent experiences. "It [the memory] is still very much with me," he admits, looking down, into nowhere. "For a good while I didn't want to have anything to do with bike riding. I didn't watch the Tour de France, nothing.

"In the beginning, I had a strong desire to ride the Tour de France, but once I got there, I had a strong desire to get away from it. Then the Tour organizers threw us out of their race with no legal right. Still today nothing changes that. They threw us out unfairly. But honestly, when it happened, I really took a sigh of relief. By that point they were doing me a favor. I just didn't want to be there any more."

Virenque arrives late at the hotel. By the time he finishes his massage, it is nearly 8:30 P.M., and most of his teammates are eating dinner. If he wanted an excuse to postpone the interview, he clearly had one. Many in his situation would have played out their option. But not Virenque. Despite the flock of autograph seekers and various other hangers-on, he instinctively asks, "Where to?"

Once inside a private meeting room, he is instantly friendly. But he is also clearly nervous. The normally high-strung Frenchman is now tense like a violin string. Throughout the conversation, his hotel room key never ceases to clink and jingle as he fumbles with it nonstop.

He speaks with force, almost aggressively. "I'll never forget that day they kicked us out," he says. "I always wanted to win the Tour. But there, it was 'la haine pour gagner,'" the hate to win.

The hate to win!

Wow. Champions often cite disappointment and frustration as motivators. But hate? Clearly, Virenque's winning drive has entered into a new realm. "I'm no longer like before. Nothing is like before."

Don't forget, Virenque grew up dreaming of the Tour de France. For a French climber, it is the only race that matters. And for a natural-born showman like himself, the Tour was his Madison Square Garden, his Carnegie Hall. But suddenly—only days before opening night in the Pyrenees—Virenque was deprived of his stage. The organizers said he could not perform.

Richard Virenque and Pascal Hervé sign in and check out the crowds as they make their post-Tour return to racing in the Grand Prix of Western France. After 200 miles the two dominated the race and instantly reignited the drug dilemma in the sport.

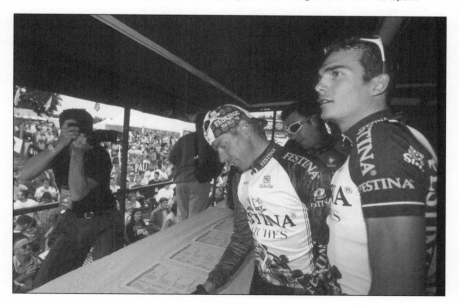

"The race organizers thought they had a bomb in their hands, and they wanted to give it a big kick to get away from it. They judged us guilty before legal authorities even made a case. But in the end, the bomb exploded right in their hands."

Admittedly, seeing Marco Pantani, a fellow climber, win the Tour, didn't help to appease Virenque's frustration.

"Honestly, I don't know how I would have done after all the accumulated fatigue and stress. But at that point, it was no longer the physical sensations that counted, it was the hate. With that kind of rage, you can often transcend the way you feel." Clearly Virenque has not earned the nickname "Richard the Lionhearted" without reason.

For the record, five of the Festina riders—Laurent Brochard, Laurent Dufaux, Christophe Moreau, Alex Zülle, and Armin Meier—admitted to taking illegal performance enhancing drugs. Stephens admits to following the Festina team medical plan, yet denies consciously taking or allowing the team medical staff to administer performance enhancing drugs of any kind. Meanwhile, Virenque's argument constitutes a kaleidoscope in shades of grey. He neither denies, nor admits to taking performance enhancing drugs.

And when he is pushed on the point, his response is abrupt. "Look, to deny or not deny means nothing. Me, I never admitted and I've never been positive. A lot of people want to label me positive. But I'm no more positive than any other rider in the peloton. I've always adapted to the rules. There were things that were said with the justice. I explained myself. Later there will be a judgment and we will know more."

Stephens, in contrast, talks freely about the recent revelations. "You know when you're in a race like the Tour, you're getting injections all the time. They say you can't drink enough, so you get IVs. Plus you're getting amino acid supplements, tablets, all sorts of things. A doctor is paid 5,000 francs a day to take care of you, so you trust him. In addition, there is a clause in our contract which stipulated that if we used another doctor and tested positive we could be off the team. So you don't look for outside help.

"You know until this year's Tour, I could vouch for the fact that you can ride the Tour de France and be clean. I know for a fact that personally, as well as through conversations, you can do good things in the Tour without taking anything. I've had good Tours. I've come close to winning a stage. And I know there was nothing going on."

When reminded that only last year he actually won a stage, his voice drops. In a dismissive manner he promptly responds, "I'd like think there was nothing going on, but I've got doubts about that one now, heh? You've got to. Same doctor, same staff."

The career-long team worker is admittedly peeved that his one day in the sun could now be clouded.

Clearly we are only at the beginning of this current doping quagmire. Given the French judicial system, it could be several months, even years, before a final verdict is rendered concerning the Festina riders.

The governing bodies of the sport must clearly define what they will accept and what they won't accept. And what they do not accept, they must be able to monitor comprehensively and completely. Anything less will only set up further embarrassing situations.

The subsequent affairs concerning the TVM team and Casino's Rodolfo Massi demonstrate the contagious web of an increasingly complex problem.

Despite the residue from the Tour, however, both riders are hungry to return. Virenque continues to rage. He dreams of winning a major stage race for the patron of Festina Watches, Miguel Rodriguez.

Throughout the whole affair, Rodriguez stood by Virenque. And today the cycling star goes as far as to say "I'm going to finish my career with Mr. Rodriguez." He hopes to have his revenge at the upcoming Vuelta and insists that, psychologically at least, he has never been stronger.

Stephens talks more simply about restoring his dignity. After suffering through three shin operations in the past year, the 34-year old veteran was contemplating retirement. "Ironically, this whole situation has motivated me to ride another season. I need to do it for myself. I owe it to myself."

In an effort to salvage his season, Stephens will ride for the Australian national team in the Commonwealth Games in September. "At this point, I'm just trying to finish out the season with a bit of dignity. That's about all I can hope for right now.

"It's funny, in the world of cycling, it [The Commonwealth Games] is a nothing race," admits Stephens. "But for me right now, to go ride for my country is about the most important things I could do. I might not be at my best yet, but trying to help a mate win a gold medal for my country, that gives me enough motivation to continue."

With some surprise, Festina Watches has stood behind its riders despite earlier threats to pull out of the sport. A press release in late August went as far as to say that watch sales around the world have never been so strong.

What's that saying? Any publicity is good publicity?

For a core group of riders, the recent events has bonded them. Virenque insists, "We feel like we've lived through something really significant together."

Stephens, however, is outside the core. When several riders copied Virenque and frosted their hair earlier in the season, Stephens decided he preferred his own blond locks. And when the team raced to their final showdown with Tour director Jean-Marie Leblanc at the Correze time trial, Stephens abstained.

Unlike Virenque, he may not finish out his career with Festina.

"Festina has been effected," admits Stephens. "The ambiance is strange. It's a great group of guys, and they are my friends, but after going through something like that, your attitude about a lot of things changes and you get kind of cold. And some of that can't help but get in between the teammates.

"For me, I still don't know what I'm going to do next year. But it's really important for me to finish out my career with some dignity. And to do that, I may need to get some distance on this whole thing. I might have to change teams."

On race day the following morning, the prodigal team received a hero's welcome from the nearly 200,000 spectators. Cycling fans around these parts are knowledgeable. But they are also passionate. And they are not about to dwell on one team's misadventures for a problem which belies the entire sport.

And once again the Festina riders put on a great show. Though under-raced and under-trained, they dominated the day. Virenque's faithful lieutenant, Pascal Hervé, jumped in the early break. Still, more than 100 kilometers remained. Behind, Virenque controlled the chase. On the final lap, Hervé dropped Belgium's Ludo Dierckxsens of Lotto, and soloed to victory.

Hervé's victory was stuffed full of symbolism. It came without the help of his head director or his team doctor. Bruno Roussel is not allowed to have contact with anyone on the team while under investigation. And Erik Ryckaert is still in jail. The victory clearly snubbed those who abandoned one of the world's top teams.

But the victory was equally problematic. Only hours earlier, the Sunday edition of *L'Equipe* announced that none of the nine athletes involved in the police investigation would be able to ride for their country in the World Championships later in the season.

Daniel Baal, president of the French federation and first vice-president to the UCI, explained, "according to the UCI rules, a rider under disciplinary investigation for doping cannot participate in the world championships."

On French television, Hervé snidely thanked Baal for giving the team even more motivation to win.

Yet as teams like Festina—as well as the equally suspect TVM—continue to race and continue to win, they persistently highlight the inability of the federations to act firmly, fairly, and quickly.

Already the previous evening, Virenque was clearly fed up with the UCI's numerous post-Tour anti-doping meetings.

When asked about the fight against drugs, he quickly retorts, "Fight? What fight? Nearly two months later, I haven't seen anything positive that has been done. Sure, there have been meetings. But for what? To look good. To look like they're doing something. But what have they said? What have they done? I'd like to think that everything that has happened will do some good. I hope. But right now that is all it is. Hope. Nothing concrete."

Visibly, Virenque has lost none of his fight.

60. Sponsors Shift Gears

THAT fellow with the boogie-woogie tie and the long face at the Tour de France presentation was Yvon Sanquer, who had spent the last four years trying to make chicken salad out of chicken feathers. Just as he seemed to be perfecting the formula, his laboratory was closed.

"Finished," he said. "It's over." He attempted a smile, which, with the loud tie, was meant to show that he was still in there battling. The long face said otherwise.

"The team is through," the directeur sportif of La Mutuelle de Seine et Marne continued. "A pity. Maybe we'll return after a season away, but I doubt it. People forget you, it's very difficult to get back to where you were. The sponsor was more than correct," he said. "They signed for three years and then gave us a fourth. But in this climate, it's impossible to find a new sponsor."

"This climate" was the doping scandal that enveloped and ruined the 1998 Tour de France and that dominated the bicycle race's presentation.

Known as the Festina Affair, the scandal was far from over. Team officials and riders continued to be questioned in the French cities of Lille and Reims and some, like Cees Priem, the directeur sportif of the TVM team from the Netherlands, had not been allowed by the courts to leave France and go home since July.

At the highest level of the sport, the reaction was still mainly talk, appeals to morality, and plans for frequent and independent medical examinations of the racers, but no outpouring of funds to develop tests that can trace the synthetic hormone EPO, the more-sophisticated PFC, and human growth hormone in blood or urine.

Sponsors, however, were beginning to move. Three French teams—Cofidis, Big Mat-Auber, and La Française des Jeux—had pledged one percent of their budgets to drug control and had established a code of conduct that dictates the suspension and eventual firing of any rider found positive in a doping test.

Another sponsor, Casino, had announced its withdrawal after the 1999 season, a year earlier than previewed.

Festina, the watchmaker that gave its name to the scandal, had taken a convoluted path: Its president, Miguel Rodriguez, said early in the Tour that if an intention to use drugs systematically was proven, he would immediately terminate his contract, which runs until 2001. But when team officials and five riders confessed to just such practices, the sponsor stuck by the racers, who resumed competition in August and publicly thanked him for his support.

Festina even boasted that the notoriety had been good for business. Then, in November, the sponsor announced that while it would keep the budget steady at 35 million francs ($6.3 million) a year, it would spend 4 percent of this in the fight on drugs, would concentrate on developing youth teams, and would cut each professional rider's salary by 60 percent. Take it or leave it, the riders were told. Some took it, some left.

Out went such stars—and admitted illegal drug users—as Alex Zulle, who joined Banesto in Spain, and Laurent Dufaux and Armin Meier, who moved to Saeco in Italy. Until May 1, all three Swiss were serving seven-month suspensions, or a month longer than Laurent Jalabert faced for calling UCI officials vampires and neo-Nazis for their handling of the Festina Affair. Richard Virenque, the team leader, who consistently denied doping despite others' testimony to the contrary, refused the cut in his 12 million franc annual salary and was negotiating a new contract elsewhere.

If his face wasn't so long, Yvon Sanquer would probably laugh at these developments. His low-budget team, La Mutuelle de Seine et Marne, was never accused of doping—it could barely afford aspirin, let alone EPO at $100 a pop.

"We never had big money," he said. "We did what we could. An experiment, that was our team. And just when it began working, the climate changed and nobody wants to get involved now in sponsoring us."

La Mutuelle de Seine et Marne was sponsored by a French health insurance company, which put up most of the annual budget of 6.5 million francs (about $1.2 million). That's small change in the sport. Budgets for other French teams in 1998 ranged from Casino's $4.5 million to Cofidis's $6.2 million. In Spain, Banesto and ONCE had the equivalent of $7.5 million to play with and, in Italy, Mapei could lure riders with $8 million.

Having so much less to spend, Sanquer worked with riders having so much less to offer. He initially built his second-division team around unproven youngsters and discarded veterans. The idea was to teach the neo-professionals, maybe win a few races, and flash the sponsor's name at unexpected heights.

Once in a while it worked. La Mutuelle was invited to the Tour de France in 1997 but embarrassingly managed to get only two of its nine riders to the finish. The invitation was not renewed in 1998.

Told long beforehand that his sponsor would drop out at the end of 1998, Sanquer curtailed the youth program and relied on veterans, hoping they would win just enough times to attract a new bankroll.

By the end of the summer, his plan began to succeed. In La Mutuelle's colors, Gilles Maignan, 30, won the French time trial championship, Francisque Teyssier, 29, won the esteemed Grand Prix des Nations, and both were selected to represent their country at the world championships. Another Sanquer rider, Stéphane Cueff, 29, won the Grand Prix d'Isbergues. At last La Mutuelle was rolling.

"Too late, too late," Sanquer said. "Maybe it would have been enough in another year, but now, where do you find a sponsor in this climate?"

61. The Next Tour

LOOKING solemn, the organizers of the Tour de France unveiled the 1999 course in Paris after outlining plans that they hoped would prevent another doping scandal and what they described as "a tormented Tour" a few months before.

"The wall against drugs has weakened in recent years," admitted Jean-Marie Leblanc, the director of racing operations, and "we saw it explode in our face."

"Cycling must regain its credibility," Leblanc said. He warned that if the organizers felt the Tour's reputation could be damaged, they would bar any rider or team beforehand or expel them during the three-week race. "If we have to start with 14 or 15 teams" instead of the expected 20, he added, "we're ready to do it."

His policy was seconded by Jean-Claude Killy, the former Olympic skiing star who now heads the race's corporate operations. "We will be absolutely hard-nosed," he vowed. "The Tour will never be the symbol of doping but of the fight against doping."

"Doping is the biggest enemy sports have ever had," Killy said after noting that a conference was scheduled in February 1999, under the aegis of the International Olympic Committee, to define doping, to establish "the most advanced anti-doping institute in the world," and to draw up a coordinated program of international sanctions against it.

Addressing the handful of riders among the hundreds at the presentation, Killy said they "were victims more than they were guilty," and "they deserved the benefit of the doubt, but from now on they can no longer pretend that they are unaware."

With that admonition, the course for the 86th Tour was made public. The words people in the sport used to describe it were "classic" and "traditional."

Starting July 3 in the Vendée region in the west of France and ending July 25 in Paris, the race will comprise a prologue and 20 daily stages—11 of them flat, 3 of them hilly, and 4 of them in the high mountains. Two long individual time trials will be held and two days off are scheduled during the 3,680-kilometer (2,286-mile) trek clockwise around France, with brief excursions into Italy and Spain.

"It's classic," said Jean-Luc Vandebroucke, directeur sportif of the Lotto team from Belgium. "Hard, demanding, big mountains."

"A good Tour, traditional, maybe less difficult in the mountains than some," said Bernard Quilfen, directeur sportif of the Cofidis team from France, which boasts far better climbers than the Lotto team has. "But, as always, it's the riders, not the mountains, who make the Tour."

"Not a Tour especially for climbers," said Michel Laurent, manager of the Crédit Agricole team from France. "On the other hand, a strong climber always wins the Tour lately, so maybe all Tours are made for climbers, even if they don't look that way on paper."

Marco Pantani was displeased. Not enough mountains and too much time trialing, he said.

"The organizers of the Tour are not making a gesture for me," he complained, ignoring the fact that the race's route is put together a year in advance—or well before it was know that he would soar to victory in the Pyrenees and the Alps.

The star climber complained especially about the final stage in the mountains, on July 21. It will include four classic climbs in the Pyrenees, including the daunting Tourmalet Pass, nearly 14 kilometers up at a grade of 8.3 percent.

"Putting the Tourmalet 100 kilometers from the finish is useless except to create extra fatigue," Pantani said. "In fact, there are only three real mountain stages, because the one that ends in Pau is worthless." The three others end at altitude, without the long descent, as at Pau, that enables other riders to make up time lost to climbers on the ascent.

Pantani was also unhappy with the length of the two individual time trials. The first, scheduled July 11 in Metz, will cover 56 kilometers and the second, July 24 in the theme park of Futuroscope, will cover 54.5 kilometers.

"Too much for a rider like me," the Italian complained. "I risk losing a lot of time."

But he made the same complaints the year before, then rode away from everybody in the mountains and hung tough in the last time trial to finish third and win the Tour by more than three minutes.

62. From Here On

BY 1998, Félix Lévitan was a frail old man of 86, a dozen years removed from his post as co-director of the Tour de France. For the first time since then, he visited the race, going to the start in Dublin as a guest of the organization.

"The size of it all," he exclaimed. He had read about what the French call the Tour's "gigantisme," but still could barely believe it. In his days, which began after World War II and lasted till 1987, the Tour was, by comparison, a mom and pop operation.

The Tour de France is indeed gigantic, which to many explained its decision to oust the nine riders of the Festina team on charges by its jailed coach that he systematically provided the riders with illegal performance-enhancing drugs. "There is so much pressure on the Tour, on their image," said Richard Virenque, the leader of the team, as he gave his version of why he had been expelled. Some of his supporters went so far as to say that it was basically a business decision.

Defenders of the expulsion argued that it would look terrible if a Festina rider like Virenque won the Tour or just a stage and then, months or years later, was proven guilty of doping. They also agreed with Jean-Marie Leblanc, the race's overall director, that sport, not scandal, had to return to center stage.

After the expulsion, Leblanc repeated that wish. "Conditions are excellent for the race," he said at the start of the eighth stage on the radio that links all cars, "and we hope that competition will once again exercise its right to dominate the attention of the public and the media."

As rhetoric goes, that itself was a fair example of gigantisme. Lévitan probably would have said, "Let's race and get this behind us." That was basically the official response in 1968 when riders protested against restrictions imposed in a doping scandal, the death the previous year of the British rider Tom Simpson as amphetamines closed down his body's warning systems against the ferocious heat on the climb up Mont Ventoux. Simpson went into cardiac arrest and died that day.

"You don't ride the Tour de France on mineral water," famously protested the French champion Jacques Anquetil, five times a winner of the Tour. Nevertheless the Tour tried to have its riders do just that. It was easier in those days for the organizers to govern: Athletes did not yet dream of seizing control of their sports.

For one reason, there wasn't much to seize. In Lévitan's time, the overall prize list was a small fraction of the 12 million French francs ($2 million) it is now, with 2.2 million francs to the winner. The number of accompanying journalists fit into a small tent or covered market place, and the loudspeakers blared accordion music, the songs of the French yesteryear, instead of rap.

In the small towns that the Tour visited, the après-race entertainment was a creaky movie projector showing films of previous days' actions as moths whirled through the beam. The official drink was Perrier, not Coca-Cola, and riders could pour the water over their swollen feet at the end of a daily stage. Lévitan's co-director, Jacques Goddet, wore a pith helmet.

In 1998 the official Tour entourage was 3,705, including 189 riders divided into 21 teams of 9 men each. There were 700 pitchmen preceding the race to distribute and sell such wares as "official" T-shirts, caps, and programs. The 700 journalists and 260 photographers and television cameramen were assisted by 830 technicians, which must mean the people who never miss an opportunity to hit reporters in the back of the head with their boom microphones and lights.

The Tour's "partners"—the Crédit Lyonnais bank, the Champion chain of supermarkets, the PMU system to bet on horse races, and Coca-Cola—had a total of 300 representatives along. Each partner paid between 17 million and 20 million francs for the right.

As "official sponsors," which paid between 4 million and 7 million francs each, the Coeur de Lion cheese makers, the Locatel chain of television renters, Crédit Lyonnais, again, and the Festina watch company seemed to have no guest rights, but their cars rolled with the publicity caravan an hour ahead of the race.

The annual budget for the Société du Tour de France, which organizes not only the world's most prestigious and richest race but also such others as Paris–Roubaix, Paris–Tours, la Classique des Alpes, and the Open des Nations on the track, is put at 250 million francs a year for all competitions. No breakdown is made public for the Tour alone and no profit figures are given, although the Tour is believed to generate several million dollars in profit annually.

In terms of publicity, reporters represented 445 newspapers in 27 countries. Fifty-six television chains blanketed 169 countries with a total number of viewers estimated at more than a billion during the three-week race. Forty-three national radio stations covered the race along with 59 local ones.

Dozens of those reporters rushed to the Festina team's hotel the morning after the expulsion in hopes of hearing the riders' reaction. Outside the turreted chateau where the team spent the night, just under the lilac climbing the walls, a sweating fan, Daniel Devors, 42, was sitting on his bicycle, a clunker that Richard Virenque would not use even to go to the grocery. Devors wore a white jersey with yellow, orange, and black flashes and the name of his club, Cyclo Varetz on the front, Agence Koenig on the back.

"The expulsion seems fair," he said, sucking in air after his climb up the long driveway. "If the riders did something like that, they should be punished. Cycling is supposed to be a clean and healthy sport."

Asked if the sport could purge doping, he shrugged. "That's the question," he said. "Nobody knows the answer."

In the town of Correze, where the finish line of the seventh stage was situated, six of the nine Festina riders met with Leblanc to seek their reinstatement. They failed.

Outside the café where the riders met the director sat Noel Dewinter, 50, who was on vacation from his financial-service job in Lille, the northern city where a magistrate was investigating the drug scandal.

"I'm not very interested in sports," Dewinter said, nursing a soft drink. "The only thing I follow is the Tour de France because it's such a great event. I've been watching it since I was a small boy."

He usually watched the Tour on television, he continued, especially the mountain stages. When he learned that the race was in the town where he and his wife were spending their annual four-week vacation, they came to the finish area to see the riders in person.

"This is a bad affair," he judged, "but you can't ruin the Tour for people. This is part of our patrimony. You can't let drugs spoil that. They've got to get this scandal over with."

But the scandal expanded, not contracted. Before the Tour was done, Leblanc and other officials had to deal with suspicion cast on half a dozen teams, with arrests and confessions and denials, with riders' strikes and slowdowns. For all his inherent decency, Leblanc was swamped. He also received little help from the International Cycling Union, the putative overlords of the sport: Its president, Hein Verbruggen, could not tear himself away from a convention in Havana when the scandal began unfolding and then went on a 10-day vacation in India while the Tour moved into open revolt.

Afterward, sporting a nice tan, Verbruggen began presiding over meetings with other UCI officials and with some riders, promising such cliches as "careful study," "open communication," and "decisive action."

Don't you believe it. These were reflex reactions by bureaucrats. Nor is it the Tour's primary job to cleanse the sport. It is, as Lévitan noticed, so big now that other interests preoccupy the organizers. (Unless, of course, such sponsors as Coca-Cola decided that the concept of a race full of drugged competitors contradicted the soft drink's image of a natural high and threatened to pull out. Do the Champion supermarkets really want their name emblazoned on the polka dot jersey worn by a rider on his way to jail?)

So, no Tour as policeman and, to judge by its quick and empty politicking, no UCI either. That left three possible censors: the courts, sponsors, and the riders themselves.

The courts remained busy after the Tour, continuing to investigate TVM, calling the rest of the Festina riders to testify, analyzing the Big Mat-Auber cache, looking into charges that Rodolfo Massi supplied his Casino teammates with drugs. A bag full of medication was found in a stream in Brive, near a hotel where four teams spent the night during the race and sent off for police analysis: Some of the nine syringes contained traces of EPO. The police had the tools, the budget, and the orders to pursue the scandal. While riders might complain of overbearing investigators, they did not seem to understand, the riders, that they were suspected of being common criminals. Their complaint that the police should have waited until the Tour was over sounded absurd, as if a burglar lamented his lost opportunities because the police had not waited politely outside the house he was looting until he was done with the job.

In the Tour of Portugal in August, meanwhile, seven riders from three minor Italian teams were banned because they failed the hematocrit test for EPO. The day after Francesco Casagrande won the San Sebastian World Cup classic, it became known that he had failed at least two drug tests in May, showing traces of testosterone; his team, Cofidis, promised that he would be fired if he lost his case on appeal. Then Cofidis told him not to race again until his case had been decided by the Italian federation. Casagrande threatened to sue Cofidis and said he would not return in 1999. Casagrande was the world's fifth-ranked rider at the time and his UCI points meant a lot to Cofidis. On the other hand, cynics said, the team no longer needed him after the emergence of Bobby Julich and the signing of Franck Vandenbroucke, who brought many UCI points with him from Mapei.

What was certain was that Casagrande, done with Cofidis, would find another employer. In their quest for publicity, most sponsors were willing to overlook anything but a rider's results. Yet so many sponsors depended on the public's trust in their honesty—banks, credit suppliers, lottery organizers, and insurance agencies—that it was difficult to believe they would continue to bankroll a dubious sport.

And, no question about it, the sport had become dubious. The most common question asked by fans now was, "How many riders take drugs?" Before, an educated guess would have agreed with Dr. Max Testa, about 20 to 30 percent, and with Paul Kimmage and Greg LeMond that the riders were marginal, people trying to hold onto their jobs. Afterward, none of this could be said with certainty. The world's top-ranked team, not a second-division bunch from Italy, had been caught, and among those who confessed to having used illegal drugs were Laurent Brochard, the world road-race champion; Alex Zulle, twice the winner of the Vuelta; and Laurent Dufaux, the winner of the Tour of Romandie and the Midi Libre in 1998 and the fourth-place finisher in the 1996 Tour. Dufaux's roommate and close friend, Richard Virenque—second in the 1997 Tour and king of the race's mountains for four successive years—continued to sidestep questions whether he had used EPO, answering that he had never failed a drug test. As everybody understood at last, that was not the same thing—not at all.

The riders, alas, still spoke of themselves as victims. Sponsors demanded results, directeurs sportifs and doctors prescribed illicit performance-enhancing drugs and what was a man to do? The idea that actions had consequences was foreign.

In general, the riders never voiced a suspicion that what many of them were doing was not only illegal but also immoral: Those on drugs were seeking an unfair advantage. To those who love the sport, only fair advantages matter. Suffering, sacrifice, and heroic performances are all fair advantages. Until the 85th Tour de France turned over the rock, these qualities were also the soul of the sport. Now those who love bicycle racing must ask, "What was I watching? Was that a rider exceeding himself because of desire or because of EPO? What makes a champion—talent or the team doctor?"

The riders must recover their honor. There will be an 86th Tour de France, of course, and many Tours after that, but never again one with innocence until the riders regain trust. The show will go on but the sport is doomed.

Index